The
Tulip Garden

The
Tulip Garden

Growing and Collecting
Species, Rare and Annual Varieties

POLLY NICHOLSON

Photography by

ANDREW MONTGOMERY

A selection of Dutch Historic breeder and broken tulips
in vintage French, salt-glazed jugs, sitting in the cool
of the coach house.

I have been growing tulips fervently, even feverishly, at my home in Wiltshire for the past fifteen years. Blackland Park (Blacklands for short) is a small, ancient estate that sits at the foot of the Marlborough Downs in southwestern England. The chalk downlands sweeping above us are rich in wildflowers owing to the low level of nutrients in the poor, sparse soil (in richer soil, they would be outcompeted by grasses), but we garden on rich, black soil – hence the estate's name – apparently the lucky beneficiaries of the sediment that has been deposited by the River Marden over millennia. This provides us with the perfect environment in which to grow a host of cultivated flowers, with tulips at the forefront. In the middle of the property sits our family home, a Georgian manor house built in the 1760s of honeyed Bath stone. Radiating from the house are a series of walled gardens and a coach house from where I run my cut-flower business, Bayntun Flowers (after my maiden name, Bayntun-Coward). The 2.4 hectare (6 acre) garden is enclosed on the northern and eastern sides by towering walls of brick and ashlar, while the river, widened into a picturesque oxbow lake, creates a natural boundary to the south. Weathered estate railings provide a barrier to the west between the garden and our flock of Hebridean sheep, which would wreak havoc should it gain entry.

Within this protected enclave I have established naturalized plantings of species tulips, such as the native yellow woodland *Tulipa sylvestris*, in herbaceous beds and meadow grass, and created perennial plantings of lily-flowered, viridiflora and other cultivars that are guaranteed to flower year upon year. Huge planters full of annual tulip displays stand sentinel at entry points into the garden, and clustered everywhere are containers of historic varieties that date back to the sixteenth century and spill out into rows of beds in a flower field within the greater parkland. My life has been overtaken by tulips, in a good way, like that of many a convert before me.

Tulips first appeared in art and literature in the Middle East almost a thousand years ago, when they were immortalized in the poetry of the Persian polymath Omar Khayyam and on Seljuk tilework excavated from the banks of Lake Beyşehir in southwestern Turkey. Those specimens, however, were representations of the original species (or botanical) tulips that grew wild in rugged mountain foothills or wide valley floors (see Chapter 1). The flower's cultivation in captivity began in earnest in the fifteenth century, when tulips were gathered in their thousands from their native habitats and introduced to Turkey's imperial palace gardens for the delectation of successive Ottoman emperors, for whom they were the ultimate expression of status and power. Their characteristic shape, generally depicted in red or (disingenuously) blue, was embroidered on garments and prayer mats, adorned the tiled interiors of palaces and mosques (most famously at the Sultan Ahmet Camii, the Blue Mosque in Istanbul) and featured in delicately painted miniatures, on leather and lacquer book bindings and in the margins of illuminated manuscripts. In these early depictions the petals (technically tepals) were shown as exaggerated dagger points, in contrast to the softer, blunter silhouettes of today's tulips, but they are still instantly recognizable as a tulip. One of the most striking tulips we grow at Blacklands, *Tulipa* 'Cornuta' (syn. *T. acuminata*), exemplifies the Ottoman-era tulip, with spidery red and yellow petals that twist and taper to needle-sharp tips.

Tulip bulbs travel well, given their small size, neat structure and protective tunic, and as the tulip continued its journey along the Silk Road into Europe it captured the hearts and imaginations of those who encountered it. Western herbalists, botanists and horticulturalists were – and still are – relentless in their quest for the 'perfect' tulip: one that is deep black or blue, has completely symmetrical markings or, today, one that can be grown hydroponically and transported seamlessly across the world as cheaply as possible. The Flemish herbalist Ogier Ghiselin de Busbecq (1522–1592) is said to have introduced tulips into Europe through his role as Viennese ambassador to the Ottoman Empire in the court of Suleyman the Magnificent (and to have given them the name *tulipan*; see below), but the botanist Carolus Clusius (1526–1609), director of the botanic garden at Leiden, the Netherlands, was intrinsic to the plant's spread across Europe. He gave some precious tulip bulbs to fellow gardeners, but was known to have guarded his coveted collection by day and night – to no avail, since it was repeatedly raided by thieves. That caused the bulbs to be dispersed across the continent, taking root and becoming endlessly hybridized by individuals hungry for the dramatically patterned broken or rectified tulips that eventually led to the economic bubble known as Tulipmania (1634–7).

For such a seemingly simple flower, the tulip has a long and complex history, and I would direct those who wish to be immersed in its fascinating story to Anna Pavord's book *The Tulip* (1999). I am a grower first and foremost, and would never be able to delve as deep as my friend and mentor has done. Even the origins of the name are confusing, for in Turkey a tulip is called *lale*. The European terms (among them Dutch *tulp*, German *Tulpe*, Spanish *tulipán*, English *tulip*) probably derive from *tülbend*, the Ottoman Turkish for 'turban', because of the obvious similarity in shape or perhaps because it was the fashion for a sultan to tuck a tulip into the folds of his head covering. To complicate matters, the tulip displays tremendous variation in the wild, confounding generations of plant-hunters and taxonomists who have struggled to make sense of so many similar, yet slightly different versions of a flower found growing in one isolated area. The early herbariums (collections of dried specimens, mounted and classified) are full of tulips whose names contradict one another from today's perspective. When I press my tulips each spring for my own herbarium – one of my favourite activities – I am grateful to those who have continuously strived to create order out of the chaos (most notably the 'father of taxonomy', the Swedish botanist Carl Linnaeus, 1707–1778), allowing me to label them with conviction – at least until the next round of classifications starts and the boundaries are shifted once more.

Tulips are today grouped into sixteen divisions (see pp.223–39, some of these are pictured on pp.24–5), which accommodate all the species and hybridized tulips in the genus, and examples from every division are represented in our garden and flower field at Blacklands. The divisions and registrations are organized by KAVB (Koninklijke Algemeene Vereniging voor Bloembollencultuur, the Dutch Royal General Bulbgrowers' Association), which operates an international register of tulip names and publishes classified lists. A few of the tulips I grow are not officially registered (for example *T.* 'Rubens' and *T.* 'Saskia', both from my Dutch Historic collection), and have therefore escaped the association's grasp, but the KAVB is an invaluable resource that I consult almost daily and depend on for my research. The many Royal Horticultural Society (RHS) resources, including the *Plant Finder*, are also crucial. In addition, old bulb catalogues, issued by such companies as John Lewis Childs in New York and Barr & Sons in England during the nineteenth century as amateur gardening increased in popularity, have also proved useful for gathering information on individual cultivars, so that profiles can be built up.

The Netherlands have become synonymous with the tulip. There, bulb companies have remained in the same family for many generations, and accumulated expertise passes from hand to hand. On a trip in 2023 to Hortus Bulborum, a living museum of tulips near Amsterdam, I was delighted to finally meet its chairman, who introduced himself as Mr Apeldoorn. I thought he was joking, given that *T.* 'Apeldoorn', a scarlet Darwin Hybrid with large egg-shaped flowers, was one of the most popular and persistent tulips of the twentieth century. But he was serious, he really was an Apeldoorn, and my belief was confirmed that tulip-growing runs in the blood, echoing the continuous thread of DNA that is passed from bulb to bulb each year.

Considering my passion for tending tulips (and flowers in general), one would think that growing would be in my blood, but it most definitely is not. I grew up in the English countryside 8 km (5 miles) outside the city of Bath (about an hour's drive from where I now live), and I don't remember seeing a single tulip in our garden or house throughout my entire childhood. My parents loved trees and lawns, but they would not describe themselves as green-fingered and had limited success at growing plants, apart from a row of rather formal flowerpots containing bright red geraniums (actually *Pelargonium*), white *Lobularia maritima* (sweet alyssum) and blue *Lobelia erinus* (trailing lobelia) – all very patriotic. As a result, my sister and I spent our childhoods gathering bunches of wildflowers, such as *Primula vulgaris* (wild primrose) and *Viola odorata* (sweet violet), from the hedgerows, for the kitchen table.

This quest for flowers has continued throughout my whole life. It ran as a thread through my university years, when I studied English literature with medieval art and architecture and would seek out flowers carved into the thirteenth-century misericords at Exeter Cathedral (I didn't find a tulip there, nor in the margins of any medieval European manuscript); through my first career as a specialist in the book department at the auction house Sotheby's, where I was drawn to gardening and cookery books; and later, when I retrained in horticulture at the English Gardening School, based at the Chelsea Physic Garden in London.

When I moved with my husband and family to Blacklands in 2007 I was faced with a series of yawning herbaceous beds, in a sequence of walled gardens within 40 hectares (100 acres) of ancient parkland. The prospect of making this my own was overwhelming for a young mother of four children, and my way of putting off the serious business of creating planting plans was to cram the borders with tulip bulbs – an approach that also meant I could fill the house with blooms the following spring. I was delighted with my first forays into flower-growing, believing the success was all thanks to my new horticultural qualification, and little realizing that a tulip bulb carries within it all it needs to produce a guaranteed display for one season. The rich black, alluvial soil played a part, but only a small one, since tulips that are grown as annuals demand little from their location apart from some sun and adequate drainage. In truth, I wasn't very interested in soil structure back then. This has changed, and I am now obsessed with soil health and the environmental aspects of gardening, as much as I am with the flowers themselves.

For a few years I was content to grow ever-increasing quantities of annual (or garden) tulip bulbs while I established Bayntun Flowers. Meanwhile, the award-winning British garden designer Arne Maynard strengthened and built on the bones of the garden, providing me with a framework within which to operate. The purchase in 2015 of a historic bulb dating from 1911, the mahogany-brown and bronze *T.* 'Dom Pedro' (see p.111), lit a touchpaper for me. I had ordered it simply because my head gardener at the time, Hannah Gardner, came across it in a mainstream catalogue and we thought it looked interesting, but this rare cultivar had a patina unlike that of any tulip I had ever seen, and I was bewitched. The hunt for tulip bulbs that couldn't be found in the usual marketplaces, but instead had to be sought out from specialists, became a compulsion that gathered momentum after my first trip to Hortus Bulborum in 2016. This obscure destination, tucked away in an industrial estate at Limmen, half an hour's drive north of Amsterdam, serves as a live database of 2,500 varieties of tulip (along with historic hyacinths and narcissus) that are no longer in commercial production. Spring had arrived late that year, after a prolonged period of freezing temperatures, and barely any tulips were yet in flower. That failed to deter me, and I was so inspired by the atmosphere and energy radiating through the 0.8 hectare (2 acre) plot that I determined to start assembling my own collection of rare tulips, albeit on a considerably more modest scale. I thought of my growing collection as a gene bank that would preserve forgotten and out-of-favour tulips for generations to come, rather like a library of rare books that spans the past 450 years, planted neatly in lines of beds like books in ranks along shelves.

Over five years I amassed enough cultivars to form the nexus of a collection, with Dutch Historic tulips dating from 1595 to the present day at its core, and a subsection of highly specialist English Florists' tulips, which were raised in the nineteenth and twentieth centuries and are distributed by the Wakefield and North of England Tulip Society. These extra-special tulips are not available to purchase (although some poor cousins bearing their names are occasionally offered from commercial sources). Instead, they are distributed among members of the society each year, and must be patiently propagated and ultimately exhibited at the Annual Show in Wakefield every May. Both the Dutch Historic and English Florists' tulips are separated into two groups: breeders, which are all plain- and solid-coloured; and broken tulips (breaks, also known as Rembrandt tulips), which are patterned with flames and feathers as a result of infection with Tulip Breaking Virus (TBV) and recognizable to many from the flower paintings by such Dutch Golden Age artists as Ambrosius Bosschaert the Elder, Jacob Marrel and Rachel Ruysch. The two groups (breeder and broken) are planted and handled separately, breeders first, as a precaution against the broken cultivars infecting the breeders with TBV.

Ambrosius Bosschaert the Elder, *A Still Life of Flowers
in a Wan-Li Vase on a Ledge with Further Flowers,
Shells and a Butterfly*, 1609–10
Oil on copper, 68.6 × 50.7 cm (27 × 20 in)
National Gallery, London

An arrangement in a Constance Spry-style mantle
vase featuring Dutch Historic tulips, *Tulipa* 'Insulinde' and
'Old Times', with *T.* 'Fire Wings' and 'Black Parrot', cow
parsley and hellebores.

By 2021 my collection numbered about seventy-five different varieties of historic tulip (both Dutch Historic and English Florists') gathered from several sources, including a group of diminutive Duc van Tols (see pp.130–35), and to make it more official I decided to apply for National Collection status. After a series of inspections and plenty of paperwork, I became the holder of the National Collection of *Tulipa* (historic) with Plant Heritage, the plant research and conservation charity. It is a great honour to hold a National Collection, but also a responsibility, as there is an onus to record all purchases and catalogue the entire collection once a year – no small task when it comes to the thousands of individual bulbs that I tend by hand to Soil Association organic standards. When I dig up the bulbs each summer after they have finished flowering and died back, I do sometimes wonder what on earth I am doing, painstakingly sifting through clumps of soil to extract every single bulb and bulblet buried within, but the love rekindles at the time of replanting in November and December and builds into a full-blown affair when the first flowers appear the following spring. Since joining Plant Heritage the historic collection has exceeded well over one hundred cultivars and we have created several more tulip beds. My passion shows no sign of waning.

Each April and May we open the garden to the public for the National Garden Scheme and by appointment to small specialist groups, in order to share the breeder and broken tulips to an interested audience – and, I hope, furnish our visitors with enough encouragement and inspiration to try growing their own at home. By maintaining the collection and sharing our knowledge we aim to help these obscure varieties to survive through generations to come. Their aesthetic and botanical appeal is immediately apparent, but they have also played an important part in the history of art, literature and economics. To lose them completely to the realms of history would be a great sadness.

As my interest in rare, historic tulips has increased, so the grip that annual tulips initially held on me has loosened, and I am growing considerably fewer of them than I did fifteen years ago. This is largely to do with my heightened awareness of environmental principles and respect for organic husbandry. The historic tulips I purchase may have been treated with chemicals during the production process, but once they arrive at Blacklands these precious bulbs find a permanent, sustainable home in healthy soil alive with microbial action. They are fed with an organic seaweed solution during the growing period, and observed closely for signs of disease; the bulbs are harvested in the summer, dried and cleaned, then replanted in fresh soil in November (for we operate a four-year rotation in the tulip beds). I propagate the bulblets they produce to build up my stocks of healthy, organic bulbs, thereby reducing the need to place repeat orders. The historic tulips work with our environmental ethos, not against it.

Conversely, annual tulips must be reordered each year to ensure an impressive bloom that is worth selling as a cut flower or displaying in a container worthy of scrutiny by paying guests. With each non-organic bulb comes a cocktail of chemicals that I am introducing into our pure, black soil, to pollute life in the earth below ground and the insect life on which we depend so heavily above ground. My solution has been twofold: to buy as many organic bulbs as I possibly can (bearing in mind that the range is still limited, and the prices high), and to change the way I use them. Instead of buying many thousands of bulbs each year for cutting and selling, I have reduced the number significantly (although it is still in the low thousands) and narrowed the range I offer, concentrating on cultivars that are not usually available in the flower markets and that stand out from the crowd: French tulips such as 'Menton' (see p.228); a range of deep, dark reds and blacks including 'Ronaldo' and 'Wallflower'; variegated and lily-flowered varieties; a few Parrots and Fringed options; and bicoloured Triumphs that mimic true broken tulips. I buy new tulips for container planting every year (sometimes mixed with a few historics), but I now reuse almost all the bulbs, rather than composting them automatically. After flowering they are lifted and dried, a selection are given away, and the rest are replanted in rough grass banks to live a new life as perennials. They won't all take to life in the wild, and their flowers will certainly be diminished for the first year or two, but I now find the natural effect infinitely more appealing. This method of recycling works for me, for the garden and, most importantly, for the natural world around us.

In line with our environmental principles, over the past few years we have started to establish permanent plantings of species tulips, such as *T. orphanidea* Whittallii Group and *T. aximensis*, throughout the garden, in herbaceous beds and naturalized in grass and gravel. Traditional plantings of bedding tulips, which are ripped out and replaced each year, have never appealed to me because of the heavy workload involved, not to mention the municipal appearance and the disruption to permanent plantings. Species tulips have a much lighter touch, weaving their way through their early spring neighbours to create subtle texture, rather than shouting for attention as do many of their hybridized descendants. Once their moment in the spotlight is over, their foliage (which is less heavy than that of the typical annual tulip) dies back under the emerging growth surrounding them, and they can be left to lie dormant over the summer months, until the cold weather kick-starts them back into growth later in the year. Those that prove too challenging to naturalize – for it can be difficult to establish them in the open garden – may be grown in containers, where conditions are easily controlled. During March and April we have a constant supply of species tulips being rotated throughout the garden in various pots, to be enjoyed at close quarters.

Species tulips are where the story of tulips began, and they are the subject of the first chapter of this book – although this is certainly not a chronological account of the genus, but rather a narrative of my obsession with this utterly bewitching flower, and a guide to using it in a wide range of garden settings in its many forms. Chapter 2 focuses on the Dutch Historic tulips we grow at Blacklands, profiling a selection of my favourites with accompanying portraits and providing detailed information on how to grow them, for they have to be treated with extra care. The same goes for English Florists' tulips, which are also part of our National Collection but which justify a separate chapter in homage to their rarity and refined beauty. Annual tulips in all their glory constitute the final chapter, which demonstrates their versatility for container displays (see opposite), as perennial plantings and as cut flowers.

I hope you find fresh inspiration within these pages, and feel encouraged to break away from the traditional tulip mould to try something new with these spellbinding flowers. Be warned, however, that tulips have a tendency to take over your life.

I

Species Tulips

A selection of species tulips, including *Tulipa* 'Danique',
T. linifolia (Batalinii Group) 'Red Hunter' and 'Bright Gem',
T. aucheriana and *T.* 'Little Princess'.

Species tulips, also known as wild or botanical tulips, are the forerunners of all the tulips that are grown in gardens today. Our collection of Dutch Historic and English Florists' tulips at Blacklands, as well as the hundreds of different annual tulips that we grow, all descend from the eighty to one hundred species tulips that have been identified to date. Species tulips are the original wild tulips from the Middle East and beyond, which have not been bred (hybridized) and so remain in their pure, unadulterated form. At one point it was believed that there were in the region of 300 different species, in part owing to the enormous degree of variation in tulips growing in their natural habitats, but reclassification has pared this down to the more manageable number. There will almost certainly be further adjustments as advances are made in the scientific study of chromosomes through the analysis of DNA. Even as recently as 2019, a new species was identified and named in the form of the yellow-and-red, slightly scented *Tulipa toktogulica*.

Our species tulip collection is a combination of pure species (*T. tarda*, for example) and species hybrids and cultivars, such as *T. humilis* 'Norah'. Many of the species tulips we grow have become so mainstream that the species name has been dropped; the tulip formerly known as *T. clusiana* 'Peppermintstick', for example, is now listed simply as *T.* 'Peppermintstick'. (*T. clusiana* is named after Carolus Clusius, sometimes known as Charles de l'Écluse, who introduced tulips to the Dutch in the late sixteenth century. For those interested in growing species tulips for the first time, this one, with its various forms and hybrids, is a good place to start.)

Tulips have become inextricably linked with Turkey, owing to their long history of cultivation in the Middle East. Introduced to Europe from there in the late sixteenth century, these elegant flowers became the emblem of the Ottoman Empire and can still be seen today as a motif in the palaces and mosques of Istanbul, where they ornament the Iznik tilework that decorates the lofty interiors. Turkey may have been the initial breeding ground of the tulip, but in fact its true home – the lands where the wild plants would have been collected in their thousands at the orders of Sultan Mehmed II in the 1450s – lies further east.

The highest concentration and diversity of species tulips growing naturally in the wild are to be found in two main geographical regions: the remote mountain ranges of the Pamir-Alai and Tien Shan (present-day Tajikistan, Uzbekistan, Kazakhstan and Kyrgyzstan) and the Caucasus Mountains, which run between the Black Sea and the Caspian Sea. In these far-flung locations species tulips make themselves at home in wide valleys and craggy foothills, where they survive in rocky crevices, sheets of scree and scanty topsoil. During the long, harsh winters the bulbs are buried in cold ground for prolonged periods (undergoing a process that botanists refer to as vernalization, see p.254). In the spring, snowmelt provides the moisture they need to grow and flower, and over the hot, dry summers the bulbs bake beneath the surface before the first rain of autumn, which starts the growth process again.

Since the Dutch nursery E. H. Krelage & Son launched a new breed of Darwin tulips at the Great Exhibition of 1889 in Paris, we have become culturally conditioned to consider the tulip as a tall, loud, proud flower that marches in serried ranks across municipal spaces and makes a brief but bright appearance in parks and gardens each spring. Species tulips present a challenge to these deeply embedded preconceptions. They are an entirely different proposition, small of stature, quiet of nature and modest in their presentation. They bring informality to their surroundings, blending in with the spring garden rather than boasting their way through it. Even the less subtle of the species have a purity and charm that are often absent in the mass of strapping annual (garden) tulips marketed so heavily to gardeners each autumn.

Despite being the original tulips, where the story began, species tulips are still relatively unknown and certainly underappreciated in the gardening world. I was already growing a wide range of annual tulips, and had started to form a specialist historic tulip collection, before I was introduced to species tulips by the plantswoman Hannah Gardner, our head gardener at Blacklands for nine productive years between 2013 and 2022. The combination of Hannah's passion for plant-hunting and wild gardening, and my obsession with tulips, led to the garden at Blacklands becoming a playground for species tulips, which we introduced across its acreage in many diverse habitats. Finding the right tulip for the right place – where it can grow as a perennial and flower year after year – has become an ongoing pursuit that has produced many rewards and a few failures. *T. saxatilis* produced a mass of leaves and barely a flower, however hard we tried to emulate its harsh natural growing conditions by planting it in an old stone tub half-filled with crocks. The squirrel population of Wiltshire has been healthily sustained by our successive plantings of *T. tarda* and sends word out across the county every time we sink more bulbs into the earth. None of this has deterred us, however. *T. sylvestris* now sways gently in the woodland beds, where it has created its own community by seed and by stolon. *T. sprengeri* is nestled among the Cedric Morris irises – irises bred by the celebrated artist and plantsman at his home, Benton End in Suffolk – in the pool border and in rough grass adjacent to the rose garden, its cherry-red flowers clashing yet simultaneously harmonizing with the bruised tones of its planting partners. Today we continue to trial species tulips both in the open garden and in containers, and in 2022 we installed a series of sand plunge beds for pots in the flower field to raise our game and improve growing conditions.

If your life revolves around tulips, as mine does, adding species tulips to the mix has the benefit of extending the flowering season by a few weeks at either end. The first species tulips start blooming in our garden in March, heralded by *T. turkestanica* and *T. humilis* varieties planted in terracotta pots and antique wooden tubs, and *T. sylvestris* in the woodland beds. The last species tulips continue to flower into late spring and even into early summer. *T. aximensis* (strictly a neo-tulipa – one that has made the reverse journey from garden cultivation to native plant – but generally classified with the species) flowers in late May, creating a dash of bright red against the acid-green grass towards the grotto. *T. sprengeri* follows a week or two later and blooms away among the irises during the first week of June. In between these early and late outliers there are successive displays of species tulips in pots, herbaceous beds and grass, covering a total period of up to twelve weeks. That's a whole quarter of a year, which is not to be sniffed at.

The environmental aspects of establishing perennial plantings with species tulips are firmly in line with our organic beliefs at Blacklands. Tulips that are grown for bulb crops in Holland

Tulipa turkestanica and *Puschkinia scilloides* var. *libanotica*
(striped squill) in a steel planter. Overleaf: *T. sylvestris* interplanted
with other spring flowers in the woodland beds near the riverbank.

have traditionally not been organic, and are routinely treated with fertilizers, pesticides and fungicides to combat any threat to the profitability of the production lines. The bulbs themselves are drenched and dusted with chemicals, and as such any bulbs I purchase cannot be classified as organic according to the Soil Association until I have grown them for a full season. The chemicals that are introduced as a result of planting non-organic bulbs not only leach into the soil, but also transfer to pollinating insects, earthworms and other soil fauna, so they have a frighteningly wide-reaching effect. If bulbs are properly looked after, species plantings should increase in size and vigour each year, rather than dwindling away as many modern hybrids do. Establishing perennial plantings, rather than buying new bulbs every year, means that fewer chemicals are being introduced into our ecosystem at Blacklands, so that I can create my own ever-increasing stock that is truly organic.

Species tulips come without the clichés of the annual tulip, the weight of art and literature of the Dutch Historic tulip (see pp.93–143) or the show-bench strictures of the English Florists' tulip (see pp.145–171). They feel fresh and new, despite being rooted firmly in the past. Until recently it was far from easy to find a good selection in commercial bulb catalogues, but distributors have now woken up to the appeal of this type of tulip, and the potential of marketing them to a new and curious audience. The main bulb companies carry up to thirty different examples, and sell them in small, affordable quantities perfect for a trial purchase, but each catalogue has a different selection, so you may have to shop around to complete your wish list. Be aware that cultivated species can appear in and disappear from the marketplace within just a few years, so buy stocks of your favourites now, build them up and you will be safeguarded against future supply shortages.

In my experience, species hybrids are best suited to being planted in pots, while the pure species look more at home in the open garden. There are a few exceptions – *T. linifolia* works well in containers, and *T.* 'Peppermintstick' looks just right in a border – but on the whole the wilder tulips suit the more naturalistic locations. This is, of course, also a matter of personal preference. At Blacklands we grow swathes of 'Peppermintstick' at the front of the pollinating border in the walled garden (see opposite), where its pink-and-white candy-stripes are mitigated by the elegance of its narrow flower head and slight proportions. It has obviously been introduced, but it looks completely natural and at home. The same can be said for *T. orphanidea* Whittallii Group in the herbaceous border above the pool, its pinkish-bronze blooms working in harmony with the fresh spring growth of perennial plants emerging all around it (see p.44).

One guiding principle should always be adhered to when planting species tulips, and that is the quest for the right environment for each. Researching where a particular species tulip would grow in the wild and emulating that is a good start, and seeing how they grow in other gardens is always helpful, but ultimately creating a thriving colony is down to trial and error. The tulip itself will tell you if it is happy, by increasing steadily in number over the years or dwindling away to nothing. Every garden is different in terms of soil, aspect and aesthetic. Individual taste is an important and often overlooked factor in gardening: plant what you love, not what you think you should be growing.

Species tulips lend themselves to being incorporated into the open garden in two ways: herbaceously (in flower beds) and naturalized in areas of rough grass or gravel. At Blacklands we have embraced both, by planting a host of species tulips in our herbaceous beds and by creating semi-wild planting zones in grass, where the terrain allows a more relaxed approach. We have so far managed to establish clumps of three different species naturalized in grass (*T. aximensis*, *T.* 'Cornuta' and *T. sprengeri*) and one in gravel (*T.* 'Little Beauty), with four varieties as permanent plantings in herbaceous beds (*T.* 'Peppermintstick', *T. orphanidea* Whittallii Group, *T. sylvestris* and the squirrel-besieged *T. tarda*).

While environmental conditions tend to dictate the successes and failures of growing species tulips in the open garden, planting them in pots bypasses this and offers more reliable results. As long as the soil mix is balanced, the drainage adequate and the watering monitored, it is possible to grow a wide range of species tulips in containers. We grow two or three dozen different types of species tulip at Blacklands each year, many in pots, adding a few new varieties every so often and discarding others that fail to flower or that simply look sad. The *T. clusiana* introductions work well for us, and we currently have four different forms, which multiply well, including *T.* 'Annika', with its primrose-yellow and peach petals. *T. bakeri* 'Lilac Wonder', on the other hand, doesn't perform reliably at all at Blacklands, which is infuriating given that it is meant to be easy to grow and is in good commercial supply (but perhaps not surprising, considering that its close relative *T. saxatilis* does not like us either).

Finally, a note on deadheading. I always deadhead my species tulips because the numbers at present mean that is a manageable task. Simply snapping off the spent flower heads before the seed heads form is a satisfying, pleasurable job and allows the plant to concentrate on spreading via offsets, stolons or droppers, which is a quicker process than by seed. There are some exceptions, however; *T. sprengeri* in particular spreads very well by seed, so I resist my automatic urge to behead it.

As we reduce the quantities of annual tulips that we purchase each year, to lessen our footprint on the earth, so we are increasing the number of species tulips that we are planting in the open garden. Plans are afoot to run *T. turkestanica* through the wildflower turf at the front of the house, and to experiment with establishing colonies in the gravel of the walled garden after our success closer to the house. In my opinion, species tulips are the future, and an exciting one.

A group of terracotta pots in the walled garden planted with
clusiana species tulips, including *Tulipa* 'Annika', *T. clusiana*
var. *chrysantha* and *T.* 'Tinka'. Overleaf: Container plantings of
T. humilis 'Helene' (left) and *T. humilis* 'Norah' (right).

Herbaceous plantings

Throughout garden history there has been a long tradition of planting modern hybrid tulips in mixed herbaceous beds, but at Blacklands we have opted to concentrate on perennial plantings using species tulips instead. There are two main advantages to choosing species tulips: their perennial nature and their long flowering season.

Species tulips are more reliably perennial than any of the other tulip divisions, and, once established, can be left permanently in the ground to flower year upon year. They also start flowering several weeks before more traditional annual plantings, as early as the second week of March, so that while Single Early cultivars, such as 'Apricot Beauty' (see p.224), are still emerging from the soil as green spikes, species tulips are already coming into flower. We first planted *T. orphanidea* Whittallii Group in our pool border in 2016 (see opposite), and it has settled contentedly along the length of this bed. It appears by stealth before the spring equinox each year, its strappy blue-grey leaves followed by a nondescript pointed bud, barely noticeable during the last vestiges of winter. A few warmer days encourage the petals to colour to a soft copper washed over with khaki; these then ripen to a glowing pinkish bronze, and all of a sudden there is a tapestry of colour and texture. The tulips stand out against a background of baby bronze fennel leaves, the bright green shoots of spurge and the first sword-like leaves of the bearded irises. The proportions all work together harmoniously and carry on in tandem for a month or more as the tulips reach their peak and the sap rises in their herbaceous neighbours. This particular tulip is extraordinarily long-flowering, holding on to its petals as they crisp and dry into late spring, long after a Single Late tulip would have come and gone.

When we plant species tulips herbaceously, we generally keep to a single variety per border, rather than creating a mixture. This simple approach seems to work best and allows them to shine. I have recently added a few *T. sprengeri* to the pool border, but this species flowers later than the Whittallii Group, so the two are never in direct competition with each other. Perhaps we will experiment with different combinations in the future, but at this stage I am so excited when a planting succeeds that I don't want to play around with it. In the walled garden, *T.* 'Peppermintstick' is perfectly timed to flower beneath the soft white blossom of goblet-trained pear trees. On a cloudy day it makes punctuation marks of pink and white throughout the border, but when the sun comes out so do the tulips, opening wide to reveal pure white petals with a contrasting indigo base. At the south side of the house is a narrow border where I plant *T. tarda*. The few that survive the squirrels and make it to flowering stage render the effort worthwhile, as the soft, yellowed limestone of the walls provides a perfect backdrop for the sharp green and white of the petals.

T. sylvestris, the woodland tulip, populates a series of island beds down by the river (see pp.36–7), where it is planted under a young collection of witch hazel (*Hamamelis* spp.) and cherry trees (*Prunus* spp.). Deciduous trees provide an ideal environment for certain species bulbs, which benefit from the increased light in spring before the trees come into leaf, and decreased moisture in summer, when the tree roots absorb rainfall, thereby allowing the bulbs to dry out as they would in their homelands. *T. sylvestris* is so well suited to our northern European climate that it is now considered a native plant in the United Kingdom, and an invasive species in some European countries.

Tulipa aximensis naturalizing in the long grass down
by the grotto in the further reaches of the garden.
Pages 48–9: *T.* 'Cornuta' alongside *Camassia leichtlinii*
'Caerulea' near the rose garden.

Naturalizing species tulips in grass and gravel

'Various species of Tulips might be naturalized by wood walks and in the rougher parts of the pleasure grounds,' noted the gardener and writer William Robinson in his celebrated book *The Wild Garden*, first published in 1870. 'In such positions they would not attain such a size as the richly-fed garden flowers, but that would make them none the less attractive to those who care about the wild garden'. Robinson's Victorian readers, brought up on showy bedding and imported shrubs, might have been surprised at the notion, but species tulips naturalized in grass at the further reaches of a garden can bridge the gap between the cultivated and the wild. In a sizeable garden like Blacklands they lead the eye away from the more manicured formal areas close to the house to the looser, more informal spaces that blend with the landscape beyond.

Arne Maynard, the garden designer who has helped us to reimagine parts of our garden, introduced us to the idea of softening the boundaries and linking the immediate landscape with the expanses of the North Wessex Downs beyond. While he did not design our areas of naturalistic species tulip plantings – Hannah and I established these together over the course of a few years – I do think he approves of the 'sense of place' we have created. In a modest space, such as an allotment or townhouse garden, the same sense of 'letting go' can be achieved by planting species bulbs in the peripheral areas, creating pockets of interest that draw the focus outwards. Arne has provided us with continuous encouragement and inspiration, while at the same time gently letting us go.

Creating perennial plantings of species tulips in a herbaceous setting is relatively straightforward, since the environment can be mitigated to an extent. The choice of companion plants, irrigation during a dry spring and improvements to soil structure are all within a gardener's reach. Naturalizing bulbs in rough grass, however, takes more of a leap of faith – but when colonies do establish, the results are spectacular. We now have steadily increasing populations of *T. sprengeri* (which we also have in the pool border), *T.* 'Cornuta' and *T. aximensis*. 'Cornuta' has settled down under some gnarly apple trees by the rose garden, its flame-like pointed petals licking through the grass each spring, steadily gaining ground year on year (see overleaf). We have planted *Camassia leichtlinii* 'Caerulea' among the bulbs, and the contrast between the red of the tulip and the blue of the camassia is striking. As the petals of 'Cornuta' slowly fade and fall, *T. sprengeri* starts to explode as bursts of bright red among the lengthening meadow grass in early June. At the other end of the garden, cherry-red *T. aximensis* flowers towards the end of May. Nestled among the wild flowers of early summer, it looks somewhat incongruous yet completely at home in a garden that is dedicated to the tulip.

There are three main considerations when choosing areas for naturalizing species tulips in grass. The first is drainage, since no tulip likes to sit in perpetually damp soil. One of our naturalized plantings is just a few feet from the River Marden, which bisects the garden. The slight incline and the quantity of deciduous trees, however, mitigate any waterlogging and the soil is free-draining.

The second consideration is the nature of the sward. Grass that is too coarse will out-compete the tulips in the long run; they will have no problem putting on a fine show in their first season, when the nice, fat commercially produced bulb forces itself through any density of grass, but problems will arise thereafter. Tulip bulbs left in the ground are nearly always smaller in their second year, and if they reproduce by offset or stolon, these infant specimens are smaller again. If they spread best by seed, the seedlings are diminutive for the first year or two. Any of these second-generation plants will struggle to work their way through a thick, coarse covering of grass and the attempt to naturalize will fail, as we found in one doomed attempt to naturalize *T. sprengeri* under an apple tree – the fault not of the tree, but of the dense grass beneath it. We trial a scant handful of species bulbs in a location before committing to it, and assess their progress before potentially throwing good money after bad. Changing the location is considerably more straightforward than trying to change the grass itself, although this can be attempted if options are severely limited.

The final consideration, which is often overlooked, is the appearance of the grass once the tulips have finished flowering. Whether you choose to deadhead the tulips to encourage offsets, droppers or stolons, or leave the seed heads on to produce seed, the stem and leaves of a tulip in a perennial planting should be left for six to eight weeks so that the plant can reabsorb energy and form a new mother bulb. If a tulip flowers in mid-April, that means leaving an area of unkempt, unmown grass and dying tulip foliage until some time in June. In the case of *T. aximensis*, which flowers from late May into June, the grass cannot be cut until August. There is nothing more beautiful than a stretch of fresh spring grass studded with the iridescent colours of species tulips on a clear spring day, but the view is considerably less pleasing in high summer. That is all the more reason to take Robinson's advice and naturalize bulbs in the rougher reaches of the garden, where they can be more easily ignored after flowering.

In 2022 we started planting into gravel for the first time, scattering a few dozen bulbs of *T.* 'Little Beauty' around the edges of the gravel in front of the house (see pp.70–1). The following spring the resulting display of little jewel-like flowers in the limestone gravel was delightful, and moreover the leaves (which are narrow and strap-like) were completely innocuous once the flowering period was over. Growing in gravel is a good alternative to naturalizing in grass, and provides the free-draining environment that tulips love.

Another new alternative to relegating species bulbs to the boundaries is to incorporate them into a meadow. The rise of 'No Mow May' has seen many gardeners resist the temptation to mow their lawns, instead allowing nature to take its course. At Blacklands we used to have a bowling-green lawn complete with neatly mown stripes, but this has grown into a meadow that welcomes spring with a haze of snake's-head fritillaries (*Fritillaria meleagris*), followed swiftly by a new planting of *T.* 'Cornuta'. The spring flowers are succeeded by waves of long grass complete with self-sown pyramidal and spotted orchids. The species tulips are only in the trial stage, and this may not prove to be the right site for them, but the environmental benefits of turning a manicured lawn over to meadow are immediately evident given the proliferation of plant and insect life. We have also incorporated 'Cornuta' into the perennial tulip scheme on the back drive (see opposite and pp.214–15), having abandoned the idea of maintaining neatly mown verges some years ago. I deadhead the tulips, then they are left to die back for six to eight weeks before being strimmed.

The delicate *Tulipa cretica* 'Hilde' is best
showcased on its own in a simple pot.

Species tulips in containers

Species tulips are infinitely rewarding when grown as container specimens. Where space doesn't afford you the luxury of planting in the open garden, if the soil or aspect of your garden precludes it, or if it just doesn't appeal, containers are an excellent alternative. Irrigation and drainage can be controlled, different soil mixes can be tried out and smaller numbers of each bulb purchased. Just a dozen bulbs of the *clusiana* hybrid *T.* 'Cynthia' in a 15 cm (6 in) terracotta pot will make a pretty focal point for a garden table (see p.73), and a few pots of varying sizes clustered together form an arresting display, markedly different from anything you will normally see in an early spring garden. When you are sitting down in the garden (if you ever sit down in the garden), every tiny detail can be appreciated at eye level, from close quarters.

At Blacklands, as a rule, we plant a different species type in each container, rather than mixing different varieties as we would with our annual displays. We keep all the bulbs for replanting at the end of the year, and want to be able to identify them at repotting time, a virtual impossibility unless they are grown separately. Given their small stature, they are also best appreciated as individual species, rather than as a combination.

T. cretica 'Hilde' (a strain of the Cretan tulip) is a good species tulip to start with, since it has immense charm, is straightforward to grow and is generally in good supply. Introduced in 1853, it disappeared from all the bulb catalogues until around 2019, when I snapped up a dozen bulbs. Standing 15–20 cm (6–8 in) tall with delicate star-shaped flowers of the palest pink, it bears up to three blooms on each garnet-coloured stem. The petals open and close according to light, revealing their surprising yellow bases in the sunshine and closing tightly at night to form neat buds. I find that a single pot of 'Hilde' is best positioned in a quiet corner all on its own, where it can shine demurely, rather than competing with neighbours.

We also grow several different *clusiana* varieties, all of which flower at around the same time and are brought out to play together. Separate pots of *T.* 'Tinka', *T. clusiana* var. *chrysantha* and *T.* 'Annika' create a joyful assemblage when they are clustered on a garden table (see p.41), their long, slender stems and narrow, unruly leaves intermingling. These *clusiana* introductions stand around 25 cm (10 in) high, in bright fairground colours of alternating reds, yellows and saturated pink, but far from being vulgar, the overall effect is one of sophistication. Their petite proportions have something to do with this, but they also retain a purity owing to the simple fact that they are all forms of the original, wild species tulips.

Another joy of pots is their manoeuvrability. They can be easily moved around according to what is in flower and what the weather is doing, and in periods of prolonged sunshine the flowering times can be extended significantly by keeping the pots in the shade. At Blacklands we keep all the species pots lined up in ranks behind the scenes until they start flowering, then dot them around the garden to be enjoyed throughout March and into April on our workshop and charity open days. When the petals start to fall we relegate them once more to the service yard. There they stay hidden from view under cover, out of the reach of rain, as they slowly die back over the summer in the dry conditions they would experience in the wild (see pp.90–91).

Our species tulips are left outside throughout the winter in a semi-sheltered position, tucked behind cold frames in the walled garden. They are subject to wind and rain and all the vagaries of Wiltshire weather, but the walled garden is a microclimate, so the temperature never plunges as dramatically as it would in an open situation. In the wild mountain steppes where species tulips originated, the temperature drops far lower, but the soil has an insulating effect that a thin terracotta pot does not. I have been tempted to keep my potted species tulips in a heated greenhouse to induce earlier flowering, but the odd trial has led to leggy growth and a less healthy appearance (*T. cretica* 'Hilde' is the exception, see p.79). Pests and diseases are far more likely to be a problem when species tulips are grown under cover, although some growers prefer an unheated greenhouse to growing outside, so that irrigation can be controlled and the hazards of wild weather can be mitigated.

Our recently constructed plunge beds in the flower field are made from railway sleepers, filled with sand and covered with a basic roof structure that protects the tulips from extreme weather and allows us to control irrigation. This new set-up has allowed us to expand our collection by providing additional space and more professional growing conditions. The sand can be irrigated, as well as the tulip containers themselves, and the water percolates through the terracotta of the pots to provide even moisture throughout the growing season. In the dormant summer months the irrigation can be halted gradually, by initially watering the sand plunge only, then ceasing altogether. This allows the bulbs to dry out completely and mimics the conditions that species tulips are subjected to in their native habitats. The sand also acts as a useful insulator, regulating the temperature of the soil in the pots.

Species Tulips for Herbaceous and Naturalized Plantings

T. AXIMENSIS

T. 'CORNUTA'

T. 'LITTLE BEAUTY'

T. ORPHANIDEA
    WHITTALLII GROUP

T. 'PEPPERMINTSTICK'

T. SPRENGERI

T. SYLVESTRIS

T. TARDA

ONE OF OUR greatest achievements at Blacklands has been to establish permanent plantings of species tulips (Division 15, Miscellaneous) in the open garden, in herbaceous settings as well as in grass and gravel. It has taken considerable experimentation, in terms of choosing the right tulip for the right place, but we now have thriving populations of eight species and species hybrids that come back every year without intervention from us. Many of the tulips listed above and profiled in this section lend themselves to other applications – for instance, *T.* 'Cornuta' (syn. *T. acuminata*) is also comfortable in our perennialized plantings of annual tulips along the drive (see pp.214–15), and

T. 'Peppermintstick' makes an exceptionally pretty cut flower – but a few seem better suited to life in the wild. I would hate to constrain the wild tulip *T. sylvestris* within a container (although I am happy to pick a stem or two for an arrangement like the one shown opposite), and *T. aximensis* needs the foil of fresh spring grass if it is to be shown to best advantage. While I am quite particular about which varieties of species tulip I naturalize in my own garden – and the garden seems to be particular about which will settle happily there – I love seeing what other gardeners manage to grow. Do not be limited by my selection, but rather use it as a starting point to find what works for your soil, aspect and aesthetic.

T. AXIMENSIS
Synonyms: *T. agenensis*, Red Tulip of Bologna, Tulipe d'Aime

One of the last species tulips to flower, *T. aximensis* (see opposite, top) catches me by surprise every year when it finally makes its appearance in late May. The large, bowl-shaped cherry-red flowers make a splash in the summer grass at the top of a free-draining riverbank, where it is naturalized, marking the end of tulip season in dramatic fashion. With pointed outer petals that gently curve backwards as they age, its rounded inner petals hold their form. It has a dark khaki base bleeding to yellow, and the anthers are heavy with yellow or black pollen. *T. aximensis* is regarded as a neo-tulipa that has been identified growing wild in only one spot – a patch of cultivated farmland measuring just 300 sq. m (3,230 sq. ft) near Aime in southeastern France – and is therefore microendemic. Its habitat was destroyed by the construction of a housing estate in 1970, but before building started a quantity of bulbs were salvaged and propagated successfully by Dutch growers, leading to a recent introduction into the commercial market. The name *aximensis* comes from the old Latin name for Aime, 'Axima'. In order to help the bulbs establish in grass, you will need to hold your nerve much later than for earlier-flowering tulips, and resist the temptation to strim until August, so that seed can ripen and the bulb reabsorb the energy from leaves and stem. We deadhead some in order to encourage the formation of bulblets, and leave the heads on others to allow the tulips to self-seed, in an experimental approach that suits the growing of these accommodating plants. This outlier is best planted in a meadow setting that you are happy to leave in a semi-cultivated state, or at the boundaries of the garden, where it can be ignored once the flowering period is over.

DIVISION: 15 (Miscellaneous)
DATE: Unknown
HEIGHT: 30 cm (12 in)
FLOWERING TIME: Late May–June

T. 'CORNUTA'
Synonyms: *T. acuminata*, horned tulip, Turkish tulip

Spidery petals of red and yellow tapering into extremely exaggerated needle points. The base of each flower head is generally pale yellow, bleeding or streaming into an intense red (see opposite, below). Petals can be uniform in shape or gently twisted, creating a contorted appearance unlike that of any other tulip. This oddity brings an exotic appeal to the garden, whether massed in a container or established in grass. Although naturalized across large parts of Europe (including the United Kingdom), 'Cornuta' has never actually been identified in the wild, and its pointed petals suggest that it is in fact more likely to have been cultivated in the Middle East under the Ottoman Empire before escaping back into the wild. In 2023 it was classified as a cultivated variety, however, given its antiquity and distinctive appearance, it is generally placed amongst species tulips. Its thin, spidery form occasionally appears out of the blue among the standard tulips in the Dutch flower fields, where it is known in the industry as a ghost or tulip thief (*tulipa dief*). 'Cornuta' exemplifies the dagger-pointed tulips that feature repeatedly in eighteenth-century Turkish manuscripts, textiles and ceramics, and it may indeed be the inspiration for this motif. Its presence in Europe was first recorded at Copenhagen Botanic Garden in 1813, and it is illustrated and labelled in Pierre-Joseph Redouté's *Les Liliacées* of 1815. I find that it tends to revert to the yellow base colour over the course of a few years, so supplementing perennial plantings with new bulbs every year or so helps to maintain its vibrancy. When naturalizing in grass, ensure that the sward is fine rather than coarse, and deadhead after flowering to encourage increase by bulblet. We plant ours in rough grass in the rose garden among vivid blue *Camassia leichtlinii* 'Caerulea' and a smattering of *Narcissus poeticus* var. *recurvus*, underneath the billowing blossom of an old 'Worcester Pearmain' apple tree. In 2023 we trialled a few bulbs in a new wildflower meadow setting, with very pleasing results, and they also feature along the edges of the drive as part of a permanent display of annual and historic tulips. I am evidently quite keen on them.

DIVISION: 15 (Miscellaneous)
DATE: Unknown
HEIGHT: 40–45 cm (16–18 in)
FLOWERING TIME: Late April–May

T. 'LITTLE BEAUTY'

Rounded heads of ogee arch-shaped petals coming to a point, strong magenta-pink in colour (see opposite). Vivid lilac base with a pale pink halo, which can be seen from the exterior of the flower through the petals. As the flower ages, the tips dry out and become papery, revealing a delicate tracery of veins within, and indeed it presses very well. Multi-stemmed with an average of three flowers per stem, clustered low to the ground. Leaves are narrow and spidery, numbering four or five. This is a very pretty and versatile form of *T. bageri*, which works well in containers and naturalized in gravel. We have established it at the front of the house, where it brightens the dullest day. When the sun shines the flower heads open out to reveal the striking markings, drawing one in for a closer inspection.

DIVISION: 15 (Miscellaneous)
DATE: 1991
HEIGHT: 15 cm (6 in)
FLOWERING TIME: April
RHS Award of Garden Merit (AGM)

T. ORPHANIDEA WHITTALLII GROUP
Synonyms: *T. orphanidea*, *T. whittallii*

Compact, rounded heads coming to a point, starting the season a pale copper washed over with khaki, developing over several weeks to an intense bronze with a pinkish tinge (see p.62). As the flower matures the khaki darkens towards the lower part of the outer petals, the tone bleeding into the top of the stems, and golden-yellow ribs become more prominent on the reverse of the three inner petals. The dark green base has a light yellow halo. The flowers never fully open or 'blow', unlike those of many other species tulips, and retain a neat cup shape come rain or shine. They hold on to all their petals until the very end of their flowering period, maintaining perfect silhouettes until the end of May as they crisp and die. Deadheading is a satisfying sensory experience, and the snap of the stem combined with the crunch of the petals positively encourages you to tend them. We deadhead rather than allow Whittallii to spread by seed, since it increases efficiently by putting out stolons. This is a very tidy tulip that would be equally at home in a small town garden or in a large, rambling herbaceous border. Even the foliage is obliging: up to four glaucous leaves clustered low down, allowing a good stem length if you are intending to harvest as a cut flower. Expect a significant variation in size over the years as this tulip establishes itself. Newly bought bulbs are of impressive dimensions and produce correspondingly large flowers; the blooms will be significantly smaller in year two, and slightly larger thereafter. This lack of uniformity creates a more natural feel in the garden, much less regimented than the annual displays of modern hybrid tulips that we have come to expect. *T. orphanidea* Whittallii Group hails from Izmir in Turkey, where it was discovered and propagated by the plantsman Edward Whittall. Its name has undergone several changes over the past century, and it can currently be found in commercial bulb catalogues listed as *T. whittallii*.

DIVISION: 15 (Miscellaneous)
DATE: First cultivated in the 1890s
HEIGHT: 30 cm (12 in)
FLOWERING TIME: April
RHS Award of Garden Merit (AGM)

T. 'PEPPERMINTSTICK'
Synonyms: *T. clusiana* 'Peppermint Stick', *T. clusiana* 'Peppermintstick', Lady tulip, Persian tulip

A new introduction of the wild *clusiana* species known as the Lady Tulip (see p.63), and one of the most similar in colouration to it (along with the slightly paler *T. clusiana* 'Lady Jane'). Candy-striped, narrow goblet-shaped flowers, the elliptical outer petals of cerise pink edged with a white band on the exterior, the rounded inner petals a solid white inside and out. Indigo-blue base that is visible when the flower opens to a star shape in full sunshine. This joyful little tulip spreads readily by stolon and seed, and establishes itself happily in both herbaceous border and grassland. It is equally pretty grown in a container. We grow ours herbaceously in the walled garden, at the front of the border in full sun, and find that it stays in flower for several weeks. It is reliable as a cut flower, and I am currently growing it at scale to supply wholesale to florists. I find it a worthy bearer of its AGM status: uncomplicated, unpalatable to deer (unlike most tulips) and unusual. It can still be found in the mountains of Kashmir.

DIVISION: 15 (Miscellaneous)
DATE: 1998
HEIGHT: 25–30 cm (10–12 in)
FLOWERING TIME: March–April
RHS Award of Garden Merit (AGM)

T. SPRENGERI
Synonyms: *T. brachyanthera*, Sprenger's tulip

Pillar box-red, funnel-shaped flowers ripening from a bright green pointed bud (see opposite, top). The outer petals are sword-shaped, their exteriors brushed with a glaze of light khaki, the inner petals are blunt and pure red. The flowers open wide into a star shape as they mature and last for at least two weeks, depending on the weather. Leaves are attractive, shiny and upright, five or six per plant. *T. sprengeri* is named after the German botanist Carl Ludwig Sprenger of the bulb company Dammann & Co. of Naples, which first put it into commercial production in the 1890s. This is the last of the species tulips to flower in the garden. It is also the most straightforward species tulip to grow, as is evident from its prevalence in the United Kingdom. Colonies can be seen in the rockery at Kew Gardens, in the Cottage Garden at Sissinghurst and on a spectacular scale at Spetchley Park Gardens in Worcestershire. This undemanding tulip is happy in a wide range of habitats and soils, in full sun or dappled shade, as long as the soil is free-draining, although you will have to experiment to find the best spot. It is a highly efficient self-seeder that flowers within four years, if the seedlings are not accidentally weeded out, and produces limited numbers of bulblets. The bulbs bury themselves deep in the soil, a habit that poses a challenge for commercial growers and explains why they are scarce and expensive. Once planted they prefer not to be disturbed, particularly during their infancy. At Blacklands we grow *T. sprengeri* in two different settings: naturalized in grass under deciduous trees alongside the rose garden, and nestled among our collection of Cedric Morris irises in a herbaceous setting. The holder of the National Collection of Iris (Sir Cedric Morris Introductions), Sarah Cook, visited Blacklands for a study day in 2020 and observed that the tulips were seeding slowly in our light woodland plantings, owing to competition from grass. She subsequently sent me a generous package of her own bulbs, which have settled among the iris rhizomes in the herbaceous border. If our beds look anything like those in Sarah's own garden in Suffolk, where bearded irises and species tulips flower simultaneously in a glorious cacophony of colour each Whitsun, I will be very satisfied indeed.

DIVISION: 15 (Miscellaneous)
DATE: First described in 1894 by John Gilbert Baker in the *Gardener's Chronicle*
HEIGHT: 30–40 cm (12–16 in)
FLOWERING TIME: June
RHS Award of Garden Merit (AGM)

T. SYLVESTRIS
Synonyms: Wild tulip, woodland tulip, Yellow Tulip of Bologna

Acid-yellow petals coming to an elegant tip, between six and eight per head (the typical number for a tulip being six), the reverse of the petals tinted red and washed with a light green in infancy (see opposite, below). As the flower ages the tips curve back and the tulips develop a wild and wayward look suitable to their status as a near-native in the United Kingdom. Stems are long and slender, with a sinuous movement that is often lacking in species tulips. Scented with a soft, spicy aroma that takes one by surprise and makes this a worthy cut flower. In John Gerard's *The Herball, or Generall Historie of Plantes* of 1597, *T. sylvestris* (referred to as the 'Tulipa of Bolonia') is described as having 'a deepe wide open cup, narrow above and wide in the bottome. After it hath beene some few daies flowered, the points and brim of the flowers turne backward ... the flower is of a reasonable pleasant smell.' *T. sylvestris* prefers to be planted herbaceously in soil, rather than straight into grass, befitting its reputation as a 'weed of cultivation' that grew among grapevines in sixteenth-century Italy, as described by Celia Fisher in her book *Tulip* (2017). We have planted it in island beds beneath deciduous trees – *Hamamelis* × *intermedia* 'Gingerbread', *Prunus* × *subhirtella* 'Autumnalis' and *Corylus* – which come into leaf or flower at the same time as the tulips and draw moisture away from the bulbs in the summer, when they like to remain dry. Among the tulips are nestled cushions of *Hepatica nobilis*, their vivid blues contrasting with the glossy yellow of their willowy neighbours. *T. sylvestris* is widely naturalized across Europe, northern Africa and Central Asia. It had reached the shores of England by 1790, when it was recorded growing in Norfolk. William Robinson was experimenting with it in the 1870s: 'tulips – I have tried only one wild Tulip, the Wood Tulip (*T. sylvestris*), sent me from Touraine to the extent of a thousand roots ... they bloom gracefully every year.' This species is highly stoloniferous, to the extent that it can put so much effort into producing stolons that it forgoes the production of flowers. Supplement bulbs by 20–30 per cent for the first two or three years to create a decent display, by which time naturalizing should be underway. I am currently trialling *T. sylvestris* from seed, having found it impossible to resist the allure of the large, swollen seed heads in late August.

DIVISION: 15 (Miscellaneous)
DATE: Recorded by John Parkinson in 1629, by Carl Linnaeus in 1753, present in England in the eighteenth century
HEIGHT: 30–35 cm (12–14 in)
FLOWERING TIME: March–April

T. TARDA

Synonyms: *T. dasystemon, T. dasystemon tarda, T. urumiensis,* late tulip

Striking star-shaped flowers of egg-yolk yellow, the tips bright white (see opposite). Long, narrow petals, the outer three washed over with olive green and a pinkish tinge that is visible only when the flower head is closed; it presents an entirely different picture when splayed open in bright sunshine. I have noted up to seven flowers from each bulb, clustered close to the ground on stems that are surprisingly short relative to the size of the flower heads. Leaves are long, slender and shiny, the basal leaf significantly larger than the rest. While the proportions sound all wrong, this popular species tulip looks very right when planted at the front of a border, where its diminutive stature can be best appreciated. *T. tarda* is distributed in the wild across extensive tracts of Central Asia, including in the inhospitable climate of the Tien Shan mountains, where it grows on slopes of rock and scree. Take this as your lead in the garden, ensuring that it is planted in well-drained, sandy soil and doesn't receive irrigation during the summer, when it is dormant. We have had problems establishing *T. tarda* at Blacklands because of continued raids by squirrels, who clearly think it is the tastiest tulip to be had. Thankfully, the bulbs bury themselves deep into the ground, and some have managed to persist and start forming clumps. We are still supplementing in generous quantities since the bulbs are readily available and reasonably priced. They are also impossible to get rid of once you have planted them in a herbaceous bed, owing to the depth to which their droppers descend. If planting in a container, be sure to tip out all the soil at the time of replenishing in November so that you catch any droppers hiding among the crocks at the base.

DIVISION: 15 (Miscellaneous)
DATE: First recorded in 1933
HEIGHT: 10–20 cm (4–8 in)
FLOWERING TIME: April
RHS Award of Garden Merit (AGM)

Growing Species Tulips in the Garden

Most species tulips are best positioned towards the front of a herbaceous border (see opposite), where their petite proportions can be appreciated at close quarters. *T. sylvestris* is an exception, perhaps – its height is such that it works well when spread across our island-shaped woodland beds. Where possible, choose a south- or southwest-facing aspect where the tulips will get good sunlight, and incorporate sand or grit into the soil to improve drainage and prevent the bulbs from rotting. We plant the bulbs quite deep (at least four times the depth of each bulb) in clusters or drifts, digging a single large hole for several bulbs and adding a few handfuls of horticultural sand (which we prefer over grit) to the base of each. It can be fiddly to plant each bulb in a separate hole, but if you prefer to do it this way, gently tip sand into the base of each hole to a depth of 2–3 cm (1 in). The deeper the hole, the less likely the bulbs are to be eaten by squirrels or pheasants, but it won't save them from moles or voles, which are real pests. Too deep, on the other hand, and the bulb may rot, particularly if you have clay soil. Water the bulbs after planting if no rain is on the horizon, although there is generally enough moisture in the soil to get the growth started.

When establishing new species tulips in the open garden, we supplement the bulbs by planting more each year – 20–30 per cent of the original order for the first few seasons – until we are confident that they have started spreading by seed, stolon or offset. Depending on the species, stolons or offsets will be produced if the seed heads are removed. New seedlings won't flower for at least four years, and care should be taken not to weed them out, particularly in a herbaceous setting; they can look remarkably like young chive leaves in the first year or two, so it is all too easy to get rid of them accidentally. If a tulip shows no sign of increasing in number after four years, it is trying to tell you something, and you would be better to dig it up and try a new position, or grow it in a container. Take care to avoid over-watering areas where species bulbs lie dormant during the summer. This is easily done when dry, but can lead to rotting of the bulbs and a dwindling display.

The practicalities of planting species tulips in grass are similar to those in herbaceous settings. Choose a well-drained site and plant the bulbs deep on a layer of sand or grit. It might suit you to dig a series of small holes by hand or with a bulb planter or trowel and place a couple of bulbs in each one, to avoid disturbing the grass too much; for larger plantings you might prefer to cut back squares of turf and dig bigger holes for more bulbs, to form a clump. Whichever method you choose, try to ensure that the pattern of bulbs is as natural and unregimented as possible. We use the proven method of throwing handfuls of bulbs down at random and planting them where they fall. Water after planting and during the growth period the first spring if it is excessively dry, then leave the bulbs in the ground undisturbed thereafter. Monitor numbers to see if the bulbs are increasing by themselves – once they start to form clusters you will know that they are there to stay.

Species Tulips
for Containers

T. 'ANNIKA'

T. AUCHERIANA

T. CLUSIANA VAR.
CHRYSANTHA

T. CRETICA 'HILDE'

T. 'CYNTHIA'

T. 'DANIQUE'

T. HUMILIS 'ALBA
COERULEA OCULATA'

T. HUMILIS 'NORAH'

T. HUMILIS 'PERSIAN
PEARL'

T. LINIFOLIA

T. LINIFOLIA
(BATALINII GROUP)
'RED HUNTER'

T. 'LITTLE PRINCESS'

T. TARDA
'INTERACTION'

T. 'TINKA'

T. TURKESTANICA

SPECIES TULIPS ADAPT beautifully to captive life in a container, in spite of their wild origins. I tend to plant a single variety per pot so that its delicate proportions and pleasing purity can be appreciated without being diluted by contrasting forms (although recent experiments of mixing the more robust *T. turkestanica* with other spring bulbs, such as *Puschkinia scilloides* var. *libanotica*, have proved fruitful; see p.35). Pictured opposite, the elegant rosy-hued *T.* 'Cynthia' is showcased perfectly in a simple terracotta pot with a pie-crust rim, and the effect would be lessened were it to be combined with another cultivar. I find it more effective to cluster pots, each planted with a different tulip, creating a living still life that can be assembled and rearranged at will (see p.41). The following pages showcase a selection of my favourite species tulips, demonstrating the variability of scale, shape and colour they offer, from the richly saturated 'Persian Pearl' and the tiny, pointy-petalled *T. aucheriana* to the loose, egg-yolk-yellow flowers of *T. clusiana* var. *chrysantha*. A wide range of species tulips are now being offered alongside annual tulips in most good bulb catalogues, and new ones are popping up each year. My favourite newcomer is the dusty-pink *T.* 'Danique' (registered in 2018). I suggest you try one or two that are new to you each year, and gradually build up your own collection to enjoy at close quarters.

T. 'ANNIKA'
Synonyms: *T. clusiana* 'Annika', Lady tulip, Persian tulip

Produces between one and three flowers per stem, each dainty head coming to a neat point when the petals are closed. Pale yellow petals flushed with peach up the central veins and at the fringes, gradually ageing to a deep all-over knicker pink (see opposite). This transformation of colour is more pronounced than in any of the other species I grow, and has led me to accuse a hapless gardener of swapping the pots around, or worse, the photographer having confused the labels. Defined base of deep purple visible when the tulip opens out to the sun. Long, slender stems and wide, strappy glaucous leaves that have a tendency to flop and crisp at the tips during a hot, dry spring. Careful staking with hazel or alder twigs helps to disguise this, as does grouping several pots closely together. I find that the scale and pinkish tones of this dainty, delicate tulip make it an ideal choice for a 20 cm (8 in) terracotta pot, but it is equally suited to a herbaceous setting. Planted at the front of a border in full sun with good drainage, 'Annika' will flower for weeks on end. Do not be tempted to deadhead. It produces seed readily, naturalizing effortlessly in the right conditions to create permanent perennial displays.

DIVISION: 15 (Miscellaneous)
DATE: 2017
HEIGHT: 20–25 cm (8–10 in)
FLOWERING TIME: March–April

T. AUCHERIANA
Synonym: Aucher's tulip

A tiny species tulip that opens out to a striking star shape, like a miniature water lily (see p.76). The rose-pink petals are semi-translucent, revealing a delicate tracery of veins within; the exterior is washed with light green. Inside the flower head the petals have a defined midrib and a pale mauve overlay. A muddy-brown base is undefined and surrounded by a cream halo, the stigma dark and the anthers laden with bright yellow pollen. I have occasionally noted two flowers per stem. Leaves are long, mid-green tending towards grey. Since this tulip spreads by offset and stolon, make sure to deadhead so that a seed head doesn't grow and consume energy best directed towards the bulb. *T. aucheriana* comes from the rocky mountain slopes of western Iran, near Tehran, but now appears to be extinct in the wild. John Gilbert Baker wrote of it in the *Gardener's Chronicle* in 1883, naming it after the French naturalist

who discovered it in 1838. It has often been confused with *T. humilis*, but is distinguished by its less defined base and smaller flower heads.

DIVISION: 15 (Miscellaneous)
DATE: Discovered in 1838 by Pierre Martin Rémi Aucher-Éloy
HEIGHT: 10–15 cm (4–6 in)
FLOWERING TIME: Late April
RHS Award of Garden Merit (AGM)

T. CLUSIANA VAR. CHRYSANTHA
Synonyms: *T. clusiana* f. *diniae*, golden Lady tulip, Persian tulip

Large heads of egg-yolk yellow and orange-red, the form considerably less narrow than the other *clusiana* introductions we grow ('Annika', 'Tinka' and 'Cynthia'). The orange-red overlay almost reaches the margins of the three outer petals, while the three inner ones remain plain yellow (see p.77). Flower heads open out to the sun to a diameter of 10 cm (4 in), up to three flowers per stem, revealing the intense yellow interiors. Base barely evident, more of a faint orange tinge. Filaments small and yellow. Confusion has reigned over the name of this species tulip. It has been labelled *T. stellata chrysantha*, *T. fernandezii*, *T. porphyreochrysantha* and *T. clusiana* f. *diniae* at various times. KAVB and the RHS have now settled on the long-winded *T. clusiana* var. *chrysantha*, but no doubt this too will morph at some stage as tulip names and divisions tend to do. This tulip is low-growing whether in the ground or in a pot, indicating that it is found on high mountain slopes in its native habitat, where it has adapted to shelter from the wind and extreme temperatures. The foliage is unremarkable and bordering on scruffy, with a tendency to brown. For this reason you might not wish to place it in the spotlight, but rather cluster it with pots of other species tulips or a selection of narcissus. I grow it alongside the scented heritage *Narcissus* 'Albatross' (1891), whose star-shaped petals and orange coronas work well in contrast. The peaches-and-cream *N.* 'Waterperry' is also a surprisingly good neighbour, a calm antidote to the punch of colour provided by the eye-catching tulip.

DIVISION: 15 (Miscellaneous)
DATE: Unknown
HEIGHT: 20–25 cm (8–10 in)
FLOWERING TIME: March–April
RHS Award of Garden Merit (AGM)

T. CRETICA 'HILDE'
Synonyms: Cretan tulip, Mount Ida tulip

Tiny shar-shaped flowers of palest pink, starting in bud with a brush of khaki-beige up the back of each outer petal that darkens to deep pink (see opposite, top left). One to three delicate flowers per stem, vibrant yellow base and stamens. Slender dark green stems bleed into garnet towards the top, and the pink-tinged, sword-shaped leaves are narrow and upright, with a single markedly wider basal leaf. It is too delicate for our borders, but I have seen it grown successfully in rockeries. Native to Crete, it thrives in a compacted, gritty soil. Ours are all pot-grown, both in the greenhouse (the only species we grow inside) and outdoors. They can be prone to aphids if kept under cover, but you can order ladybirds from a biological pest-control company (see p.255). They increase effectively by offset.

DIVISION: 15 (Miscellaneous)
DATE: 2017
HEIGHT: 15–20 cm (6–8 in)
FLOWERING TIME: March

T. 'CYNTHIA'
Synonyms: *T. clusiana* 'Cynthia', Lady tulip, Persian tulip

The result of a cross between the yellow and white forms of *T. clusiana*, this tulip presents as a toned-down version of *T.* 'Tinka', the base colour a paler yellow and the red overlay a softer orange-pink (see opposite, below left). As with 'Tinka', the contrasting red is confined to the three outer petals, while the three inner ones remain pure yellow. Long, narrow flower heads proportionately large to the height of the stems; long-lasting as a cut flower. Narrow grey-green leaves upright, slender and self-supporting. I plant small potfuls each year and position them around the greenhouse and conservatory just as they come into flower; they don't do well in the house, given the heat from our log fires. It is rarely necessary to buy new bulbs, since decent-sized offsets are produced each year. Being container-grown, they are easy to harvest and pot up in fresh soil. I have seen 'Cynthia' naturalized in grass, but that sward was poor; this tulip would not like competition from a healthy lawn.

DIVISION: 15 (Miscellaneous)
DATE: 1959
HEIGHT: 20–25 cm (8–10 in)
FLOWERING TIME: March–April
RHS Award of Garden Merit (AGM)

T. 'DANIQUE'

This is a delightful species hybrid, of recent introduction, that has one largeish flower head often accompanied by a second or third small flower on a shorter stem (growing from the uppermost leaf joint, see opposite, top right). It is therefore described as multi-stemmed, although it does not obviously appear so. The dusty-pink flowers are best appreciated when open, so that they reveal an inky-blue base with a halo of creamy yellow; the same shade of yellow extends up the midribs of the three inner petals. A square profile at the base morphs into a cup-shaped form. Anthers are large and brown, rising from narrow filaments around a tiny, pale stigma. Narrow mid-green leaves are mottled dark pink on their backs and have pink tips. In 2023 I won the Species Tulip class at the Tulip Society Annual Show with a vase of five stems of 'Danique'.

DIVISION: 15 (Miscellaneous)
DATE: 2018
HEIGHT: 30–35 cm (12–14 in)
FLOWERING TIME: Late April

T. HUMILIS 'ALBA COERULEA OCULATA'
Synonyms: *T. albocaerulea* Oculata Group, *T. humilis* var. *pulchella* Albocaerulea Oculata Group

An exceedingly pretty tulip that justified my long quest for its bulbs. Delicate white petals, narrow at the base, wider in the middle, extending to a point (see opposite, below right). The exterior of the three outer petals is washed with lime-green, with surprising pink tips. The pointed shape of the petals is echoed in the pattern of the indigo-blue base on the interior of the flower. Anthers are dark indigo, dusted with yellow pollen, and the stigma pink. The four or five leaves are neat in form, slightly shorter than the stem, adding to the tulip's tidy appearance. Its petite proportions do not lend themselves to naturalizing so we grow it in small terracotta pots. It can be kept in a cold frame or unheated greenhouse, protected from wind and rain. New bulbs may be mean in size; our first purchase produced small flowers and took a couple of years to bulk up and produce correspondingly larger blooms.

DIVISION: 15 (Miscellaneous)
DATE: First recorded in 1927 by Georg Egger
HEIGHT: 15 cm (6 in)
FLOWERING TIME: March–April

T. HUMILIS 'NORAH'
Synonym: *T.* 'Norah'

Bubblegum-pink goblet-shaped flowers, the colour a little cloying for some (see opposite). The intensity of the pink is relieved by a green rib on the reverse of the outer petals and a striking base of charcoal bleeding to indigo, then white; this occupies more than a third of the inside of the flower, and makes it distinctive and easy to identify. Petals taper to a point and open out to a star shape in strong light. Stems are short, not particularly strong and prone to growing towards the light, so if you like uniformity, keep turning the pots to maintain a more upright and even growth habit. Grey-green leaves are grooved and proportionately long in relation to the length of stem. They remain healthy-looking throughout the growing period, with no browning or crisping at the tips. I tend to grow 'Norah' in pots, but it is quite forgiving whether grown in a container or in open ground, tolerating a range of soil conditions and even putting up with wet British summers. However, like most species tulips, it prefers to be kept dry in the summer, so if you plant this hybrid herbaceously, ensure that it is grown among plants that do not require irrigation. Bearded irises make a suitable companion. 'Norah' is a hybrid of *T. humilis* (syn. *T. aucheriana*), which hails from the Middle East and was introduced to England in 1844. *T. humilis* is part of the Saxatilis group of species tulips, all of which have pinkish flowers. I find this particular hybrid easier to grow than *T. saxatilis*, which likes its roots to be very constricted and provides me with many bulblets but maddeningly few flowers.

DIVISION: 15 (Miscellaneous)
DATE: 2017
HEIGHT: 15–20 cm (6–8 in)
FLOWERING TIME: Late March

T. HUMILIS 'PERSIAN PEARL'
Synonym: *T.* 'Persian Pearl'

Vibrant magenta, the three outer petals are considerably more slender than the three inner ones, and washed in streaks of silvery green (see p.82). Petal numbers vary, and I find that my examples of 'Persian Pearl' sometimes have four larger inner petals. Stamens can also be irregular in number. The egg-yolk-yellow base creates a pleasing contrast with the magenta of the petals, particularly on a sunny day, when the flower head opens out to a star shape. Long, linear grey-green leaves stay upright and fresh-looking throughout the flowering period, a trait that is common to all the *humilis* tulips I grow. The only drawback with this tulip is the tendency for its petals to become badly marked by rain or hail (I dread a March hailstorm more than any other weather phenomenon). Other *humilis* cultivars, such as 'Norah' or *T. humilis* 'Alba Coerulea Oculata', are more forgiving, but the intense saturation of colour in 'Persian Pearl' renders it especially vulnerable. I certainly wouldn't want to grow it in the open garden where shelter could not be provided, despite the fact that it is a good naturalizer.

DIVISION: 15 (Miscellaneous)
DATE: 1974
HEIGHT: 10 cm (4 in)
FLOWERING TIME: March–April

T. LINIFOLIA
Synonyms: *T. batalinii*, *T. maximowiczii*, flax-leaved tulip

Deeply saturated scarlet flowers ending in a neat point, the three inner petals upright, the three outer reflexed at the tips (see p.83). Bulbous when closed, bowl-shaped when open, the base is smudged into the lower portion of the petals. Stamens are dark purple and slender with very long, narrow anthers. Grey-green thin leaves, mostly at the base of the stem, with slightly undulate margins (although not in all cases). Pleasantly scented, with a glossy sheen to the inside when open to the sun. *T. linifolia* still appears to be widely distributed in the wild (chiefly in Afghanistan and Tajikistan), although – in common with many species tulips – it has come under threat from over-picking and over-grazing. This is hardly surprising considering its colour, which makes it a conspicuous target for humans and animals alike. It is a good choice for an English garden, since it copes with the rainfall and damp soils that are associated with a maritime climate. I find the colour too vibrant to let loose in the garden, so I keep it in pots. A dozen bulbs make a dazzling display, which lasts well. The yellow form of *T. linifolia* was previously known as *T. batalinii*, and is now generally listed under *T. linifolia* Batalinii Group.

DIVISION: 15 (Miscellaneous)
DATE: Unknown
HEIGHT: 15–20 cm (6–8 in)
FLOWERING TIME: April
RHS Award of Garden Merit (AGM)

T. LINIFOLIA (BATALINII GROUP) 'RED HUNTER'
Synonym: *T.* 'Red Hunter'

Tomato-red flowers, the three interior petals brighter in colour and coming to a pronounced point, the three exterior ones slightly duller and washed with a greenish tinge until the flower head is fully mature (see opposite, top left). A small base of inky black contrasts wonderfully with the glossy red of the petals; the dark stamens are neat and upright, the stigma white. The stem holds itself upright with no need for twiggy supports, and the grey-green leaves keep their form obligingly as the plant develops. I enjoy growing this hybridized species tulip in contrast to the original *T. linifolia*, and find that it has a distinctly cultivated, constrained appearance, as though it belongs in the garden, not the wild. 'Red Hunter' was one of the plants selected to mark the bicentenary of the RHS in 2004, and it is easy to see why – it is the perfect little red tulip.

DIVISION: 15 (Miscellaneous)
DATE: 1993
HEIGHT: 20–25 cm (8–10 in)
FLOWERING TIME: Late April
RHS Award of Garden Merit (AGM)

T. 'LITTLE PRINCESS'
Synonym: *T. hageri* 'Little Princess'

Coppery-red flowers are borne in loose clusters of three or four pointy-petalled blooms per stem (see opposite, below left). The three outer petals are tinged green towards the bottom, the rest of the petal a darker copper than the three inner (which have a blood-red central rib). The star-shaped base is charcoal, edged with a band of golden yellow. Strap-like, mid-green leaves hold their shape nicely. This is a very straightforward tulip, easy to grow in containers or naturalized in the garden. It will happily perennialize given the right free-draining conditions, and is a striking alternative to *T. orphanidea* Whittallii Group in a herbaceous setting.

DIVISION: 15 (Miscellaneous)
DATE: 1991
HEIGHT: 20 cm (8 in)
FLOWERING TIME: Late April
RHS Award of Garden Merit (AGM)

T. TARDA 'INTERACTION'
Synonym: Late tulip

All the components of this delightful, decorative tulip work together as a study in shades of green, yellow and white (see opposite, top right). Narrow goblet-shaped flower heads have outer petals of greyish green with a pink tinge, contrasting with inner petals of a pale yellow blending to white towards the tips. The interior is a pure bright yellow with no base, and narrow white margins to the petals. Stamens and stigma are of a similar yellow and therefore barely noticeable. Leaves are erect, variegated grey-green with a white band and pretty pink rim. While the origins of 'Interaction' can be seen in *T. tarda*, the hybrid is far more ornamental and user-friendly; the flower head holds its shape in the sun rather than blowing right out, the stems are longer, the foliage pleasing. While I would not want it in the open garden at Blacklands, where it would appear out of place, this brand-new introduction is worth looking out for, and I will continue to plant it in small terracotta pots.

DIVISION: 15 (Miscellaneous)
DATE: 2022
HEIGHT: 20 cm (8 in)
FLOWERING TIME: Late April

T. 'TINKA'
Synonyms: *T. clusiana* 'Tinka', Lady tulip, Persian tulip

Another cultivar of *T. clusiana*, with slender heads of lemon yellow overlaid with a large red diamond (see opposite, below right). Any vulgarity is tempered by the delicacy of this pretty little tulip, which sits on long, slender stems. The three inner petals are solid yellow, the outer three bicoloured red and yellow on the reverse. Stamens are dark purple but generally hidden, since 'Tinka' does not open fully. Many very slender glaucous to silver-green leaves, benefiting from twig supports to keep them from collapsing. I prefer to grow 'Tinka' in pots. Much fun can be had from the effect of up to thirty bulbs planted in a 30 cm (12 in) terracotta pot, or a dozen each in 15 cm (6 in) pots arranged in a group (see p.41) or along an outside dining table. Remember to turn the pots regularly to prevent the flowers from growing towards the sun.

DIVISION: 15 (Miscellaneous)
DATE: 1994
HEIGHT: 25–30 cm (10–12 in)
FLOWERING TIME: March–April
RHS Award of Garden Merit (AGM)

T. TURKESTANICA
Synonym: Turkestan tulip

Little star-shaped cream flowers with yellow centres burst into flower in early March (see opposite), the second of the species tulips to flower in our garden every spring (after *T. humilis*). This is not a showy tulip, given its subtle colouration and delicate flowers, but it is most generous: multi-flowered with up to nine flower heads, branching out in a cluster from the top of the stem. The backs of the outer petals are washed with a greyish green. Two wide glaucous leaves are taller than the flower itself, but do not dominate its overall appearance. I have seen examples elsewhere with additional leaves that are narrow and grooved. We plant *T. turkestanica* massed as a single species in containers or mixed with other spring bulbs and perennials; they look particularly appealing combined with *Puschkinia scilloides* var. *libanotica* (with star-shaped flower heads that echo those of the tulip, see p.35) and hellebores, with a few ferns for texture. I have tried growing these tulips in a heated greenhouse (they become leggy) or bringing them into the house once they are in flower (they flop dramatically), so I now keep the containers outside, moving them to a sheltered position in windy weather. In 2022 we started scattering a few of the bulbs through the pool border, where they are a welcome precursor to the *T. orphanidea* Whittallii Group that have been naturalized there for some years. Within a few years they should bulk up to form clumps. *T. turkestanica* hails from the foothills of the Pamir-Alai and Tien Shan mountain ranges of Kyrgyzstan, Kazakhstan and Uzbekistan, but does well in the maritime climate of the United Kingdom, where it is able to survive in a range of soils, including those with a moderate clay content.

DIVISION: 15 (Miscellaneous)
DATE: Recorded by Eduard August von Regal in 1875
HEIGHT: 20–30 cm (8–12 in)
FLOWERING TIME: March
RHS Award of Garden Merit (AGM)

A container planting of *Tulipa humilis* 'Norah', with twigs of
alder (*Alnus glutinosa*) from the garden to provide support.

Growing Species Tulips in Containers

Planting is best undertaken from the start of November, and we try to complete it by mid-December. Late planting results in later flowering, and half the point of growing species tulips is to have an early show. We use a homemade recipe of equal parts of our own loam (which is very free-draining), an organic multipurpose (peat-free) potting compost and sand. Use plenty of crocks at the bottom of the pot, backfill with the soil mix and place the bulbs about halfway down the pot, or at least three times their depth. As long as your potting mixture contains sand and is free-draining, there is no need to place the bulbs on a layer of sand. A thin layer of grit smoothed over the surface of the soil makes a satisfying finish and prevents soil from splashing up the edges of the pot after rain or watering. Irrigate straight after planting and regularly during dry spells. Once the tulips are in full growth, they should be fed with a dilute seaweed formula every two weeks. If the tulip starts flowering from a very short stem so that it appears to be blooming straight out of the soil, it can mean it needs more water. Either sit the pot in a tray of water or use a watering can with a spout (rather than a rose attachment) and concentrate the flow around the rim of the pot. Watering directly onto the flower itself can cause the petals to mark and scorch them on a sunny day.

Squirrels are the number-one enemy for bulbs growing outside, and to combat this we place an individual conical chicken-wire 'hat' over each pot straight after planting. This remains in place until the furled leaves start pushing through, by which time the squirrels will have found food elsewhere. Rats and mice can also cause trouble, but battery-operated sonar deterrents are very effective against them. Deer can be a nightmare where tulips are concerned, and tall fences are the only real solution. Happily, we don't have a problem with this particular pest since our garden is surrounded by high walls, old estate railings and the River Marden.

Once the leaves are through and the chicken-wire hats have been removed, it is time to consider staking. The smaller, neater species tulips, such as *T. cretica* 'Hilde' and *T. humilis* 'Norah', never require support, but the taller *clusiana* varieties can benefit from it, unless you don't mind them flopping over the edges of the pot. Bare winter branches of alder or hazel are my favourite choice of staking material (see opposite), but twiggy branchlets of any deciduous tree will work.

After the species tulips have finished flowering, deadhead them to prevent seed formation, and give them one last water with a dose of feed. This is when the fact that they are grown in pots really comes into its own, since you will be able to move them to a hidden corner and ignore them throughout the summer. As the leaves and stems die back, the energy is reabsorbed into the formation of a new bulb, which will flower the following spring (see overleaf). In autumn, empty the accumulated pots and retrieve the bulbs, taking care to extract any new bulblets from the soil or any droppers that might be hiding at the bottom. The small new bulbs can be potted up separately to flower a couple of years hence, but be careful not to accumulate more than you can realistically care for. I always think that I must keep every single bulblet, but after a recent trip to the collections at Kew and the Cambridge University Botanic Garden – both of which have sensible quantities of each species – I realized my habit was getting out of control, and subsequently thinned down my collection to make it more manageable. I found no shortage of gardening friends happy to take a few bulbs to try growing themselves.

When replanting the bulbs, don't be tempted to recycle the old soil. It will be spent, so it really is worth making a fresh, nutrient-rich soil mix every year in order to maintain the health and vigour of your tulips. The aim is for the bulbs to come back perennially without the need to buy in new stock each year, although in my experience new introductions in the late summer bulb catalogues can prove hard to resist.

II

Dutch Historic Tulips

A vintage jug with the old Cottage tulip *Tulipa* 'Old Times',
the mahogany-brown breeder *T.* 'Dom Pedro' (lower right)
and the deep purple breeder *T.* 'Klopstock'.

The Dutch Historic tulip collection at Blacklands comprises around one hundred different cultivars dating from the late sixteenth century to the present day, and is formed of tulips that are rare, unusual and not generally available commercially. The collection is divided into breeder (plain tulips, uninfected by Tulip Breaking Virus) and broken tulips (decorative, patterned petals caused by the virus), with a sub-collection of the diminutive, brightly coloured Duc van Tol cultivars. 'Dutch Historic' is something of a misnomer, since it covers tulips that were bred in the Low Countries, France and even England, but it has become the accepted label for a wide-ranging collection such as this, owing to the pre-eminence of the Netherlands in the tulip industry from the late sixteenth century until the present day.

I add to the collection every year with carefully sourced purchases and am guided by what is available on the open market, what I am offered through private collectors and what appeals to me most strongly. Small, demure tulips, such as 'Lac van Rijn' (1620), excite me because of their antiquity, but I am also drawn to the jewel-like Duc van Tol cultivars, double Peony types, such as 'Yellow Rose' from c.1700, and the cluster of Single Early breeders that were introduced around 1900: such varieties as 'Queen Alexandra' (1900) and 'Feu Ardent' (1907) in deeply saturated, brooding colours. Broken (also known as rectified) tulips marbled with one or more rich shades are the most alluring of all. I am not the first to fall under their spell, and I won't be the last. Where there are chronological gaps in my collection, I endeavour to fill them without being slavish, and when I am passionate about a particular group I seek out as many different variations as I can. The Dutch Historic collection will never be fully comprehensive; instead, it offers a wide-ranging representation of some of the most arresting and interesting tulips bred over the past 400-plus years, as seen through my eyes.

The first historic tulip I ever ordered, in 2015, was 'Dom Pedro' (1911), a deep mahogany-brown breeder with a vivid yellow base. It had a presence that I had never previously encountered in a tulip, radiating antiquity and depth in much the same way as a piece of antique furniture that has been burnished to a shine over many generations. This seemingly innocent purchase triggered a dangerous shopping habit that was entirely removed from the casual flicking-through of bulb catalogues that I had previously enjoyed.

The earliest tulip in our Dutch Historic collection is the diminutive 'Duc van Tol Red and Yellow', dating back to c. 1595, when it was known to have been grown by Carolus Clusius at the botanic garden in Leiden, the Netherlands. Its petals of scarlet edged in cadmium yellow are wide at the base and curve into sharply pointed tips. Records of its breeding are not extant, as is the case with many of the older tulips, so it is not known whether it was brought as a bulb from the East or bred in the Netherlands. Whatever the case, it is representative of the needle-petalled tulips that were in vogue throughout the Ottoman Empire in the late fifteenth and sixteenth centuries, and is a good example of a Dutch Historic tulip at the opening chapter of the story. The dainty 'Lac van Rijn', with white-edged petals of pinkish purple, exhibits a similar pointy-petalled form, as does the pure white 'Alba Regalis' (said to date from 1620 or 1670). Both have a quiet but prominent presence in our collection.

While there may be no surviving records of where these early cultivars were bred, or by whom, there are plenty of detailed visual records in the form of Dutch Golden Age still life paintings or *bloemenstillen*. It gives me endless satisfaction to identify 'Lac van Rijn' in such paintings as *A Still Life of Flowers in a Wan-Li Vase on a Ledge with Further Flowers, Shells and a Butterfly* by Ambrosius Bosschaert the Elder (1609–10, indicating that 'Lac van Rijn' is earlier than is commonly perceived; see p.23), and I am frequently to be heard exclaiming 'Look at that Duc van Tol!' or 'That must be a Peony Rose!' while peering closely at paintings in galleries and museums the world over. I also offer a good sideline in identifying tulips for auction houses and art dealers. Sadly, hardly any of these very early tulips survive. A study of first editions of *Hortus Eystettensis* by Basilius Besler (1613) and *Paradisi in Sole Paradisus Terrestris* by John Parkinson (1629) reveals woodcuts of dozens of different cultivars, almost all of which have become extinct. Considering that the survival of these old cultivars depends on a genetic line having been maintained bulb after bulb over almost half a millennium, it is hardly surprising that so few remain.

The broken flamed and feathered varieties that fuelled the period known as Tulipmania in 1634–7 have become as elusive as their unbroken counterparts. The most renowned of all tulips, 'Semper Augustus', exists now only in print and paint, but the 'Silver Standard' that we grow at Blacklands, dating from 1760, is highly evocative of it, with striking crimson markings flickering over a white base. 'Silver Standard' is the earliest broken tulip in our collection, preceded chronologically by a dozen or so different breeders. There is a reason behind the scarcity of the oldest broken tulips, and this lies in the cause of the markings that have always made them so alluring: Tulip Breaking Virus.

Tulip Breaking Virus (TBV) is a potyvirus that was discovered by the mycologist Dorothy Cayley in 1927. It is spread by aphids, which feast indiscriminately on (infected) broken flowers and (uninfected) unbroken ones, spreading disease wherever they land. Within a calendar year this virus can infiltrate a stock of breeder or unbroken bulbs in the ground or in storage, turning a valuable crop of plain tulips into a field of streaked and striated misfits. The last thing a tulip-grower in the Netherlands can afford is for a valuable crop of plain supermarket-style tulips to be infected with TBV and rendered worthless. Old broken tulips that play host to the virus have become completely outlawed by the industry. It is now illegal to grow them in the Netherlands, save for historical purposes, and they can be found only at such sites as the Hortus Bulborum, where the display is spectacular, and in the gardens at Keukenhof, where they are planted in beds but make a rather meagre show at the end of the season.

The same virus that causes a breeder tulip to rectify into a painterly broken flower can also weaken the bulb over time, resulting in a lack of vigour in terms of both its reproductive potential and its vitality as a flower. I find that a broken variety – 'Bridesmaid' (1900), for example – might produce a decent new mother bulb and perhaps a single small offset (bulblet) by the time it is lifted in July, whereas a breeder tulip of the same date – 'Queen Alexandra', for instance – might produce twice as many offsets, all of decent flowering size. With such a lack of supply it is easy to see how stocks of even the most flamboyantly desirable tulips could dwindle to nothing, and why so many of the varieties immortalized in seventeenth-century Dutch and Flemish oil paintings can no longer be traced.

Tulipa 'Lac van Rijn' is a delicate tulip and one of the
earliest cultivars in our collection, dating from 1620.
Overleaf: *T.* 'Silver Standard' (front) and 'Striped Sail'
bloom in raised beds in the flower field.

Dutch Historic breeder tulips planted in a raised bed
in the flower field, including *Tulipa* 'Bleu Aimable',
'Admiral Tromp' and 'Dillenburg'.

Shortage of stock was one of the factors that caused the tulip 'bubble' to burst in 1637, when demand outstripped supply many times over for a short period. A mere twelve bulbs of 'Semper Augustus' were ever recorded, and a single bulb was worth ludicrous sums of money, allegedly as much as a grand townhouse on the most prestigious canal in Amsterdam. There is also evidence to suggest that tulips became an increasingly unpopular commodity after the speculative market collapse that signalled the end of Tulipmania, owing to the havoc they had inadvertently wreaked on the economy and the livelihoods of those who had invested so much in it. The tulips that had previously been guarded day and night to prevent opportunistic theft suddenly became a liability, and were metaphorically and literally consigned to the compost heap.

While breeder tulips may not have succumbed to the fate of those infected by TBV, they have not been immune to the vagaries of the tulip industry. Some Dutch Historic tulips, such as 'Lac van Rijn', have fallen out of fashion, perhaps because they are often small in stature and flower very late in the season. In today's world, size, novelty and transportability dictate the cut-flower market. Commercial tulips are invariably grown under cover and forced in state-of-the-art operations. Carefully controlled levels of artificial light, heat and chemical feed are orchestrated to bring them into flower early in the new year, and as a result consumers have come to think of tulip season as lasting from January until March. By late April or May they are considered yesterday's flowers, and the public has become hungry for the full blooms of summer – just when the historic tulip is coming into its own. As our annual tulip displays at Blacklands draw to a close towards the end of April, the historic tulips take the baton and flower on into May. Attempts by the industry to precipitate flowering of the old varieties have generally been unsuccessful (the Duc van Tols being an exception; see p.130), and their popularity has waned in indirect proportion to advances in technology.

In the same vein, as cut flowers have become an international commodity, the delicate older tulips have lost their footing in the industry. The larger and more robust a tulip is, the better it can withstand transportation and refrigeration, and the more profitable the crop. Little 'Lac van Rijn' would not fare well if it were packed and despatched around the world, nor would it cry out to be ordered in competition with the plethora of tulips on offer in the bulb catalogues. Small, late-flowering, old-fashioned varieties have for the most part been banished to history or to historic collections, but it is this rarity that is part of their appeal. Their late flowering is a bonus for me, since it extends the tulip season by a few weeks.

It is evident why some of the tulips in our Dutch Historic collection have become rare to the point of extinction, but we grow others that present no obvious reason for their scarcity, save for changes in taste over the centuries. The world of tulips is a fickle one, and a particular variety can be all the rage for a spell, only to sink into obscurity thereafter. 'Je Maintiendrai' (1863) is one example that surely deserves a resurgence in popularity. It is an elegant cup-shaped, Single Late breeder, enduring in flower with tones of burnt copper and amethyst blending beguilingly into each other. Being a breeder, it presents no risk of spreading TBV, and produces a healthy number of offsets while maintaining the size of the mother bulb. Visitors to my flower field always remark on it, and the few precious stems I sell to London florists are much admired.

Another of my favourite breeders, 'Madras' (1913), is a stately Single Late variety of lightly burnished copper flushed with cerise. It caused a stir when it was reintroduced in selected catalogues a few seasons ago, only to disappear once more. Having ordered a couple of dozen bulbs one year, we greedily ordered a hundred or so the next. They came up a shocking pillar box-red, and we have been trying to eliminate them from our beds ever since. This can happen when a tulip suddenly becomes popular; unable to keep up with demand, the bulb companies substitute inferior and sometimes completely different bulbs to satisfy orders. I continue to keep an eye out for 'Madras' and take the risk of ordering it in modest numbers, in the knowledge that it might not be what I was expecting.

A few of the old broken varieties have reappeared in the marketplace over the past few years, because their bulbs have proved to be unaffected by the ill effects of TBV, remaining strong and vigorous. More research is required in the field, but it seems that the virus has been absorbed and stabilized within the DNA of these tulips, so that we get the positive effects without any weakening of the bulb – and, perhaps most importantly, without the threat of TBV infection. 'Absalon' (1780) and 'Insulinde' (c.1915) are two broken cultivars that thrive in our Dutch Historic collection. They are an excellent starting point for a collection of this kind, being exquisitely beautiful, straightforward to grow and moderately easy to obtain. The fact that they produce several offsets and therefore increase each year adds to their appeal, and means that I am always happy to cut the odd stem for the house.

Not as steeped in history, but beguiling in their own right, are selectively bred imitations of the original broken varieties. If you ever see bulbs of 'Inner Wheel' for sale, buy as many as you can possibly afford. Originally introduced to the market by Frans Roozen in 1987 as a Single Late, it has since 2008 been available in its broken state as a spectacular modern Rembrandt. Tall and long-lasting with swirling shades of deep pink, carmine red and purple on a cream ground, it appears more antique than its dates imply. Despite being of such recent vintage, it is a welcome member of the collection at Blacklands and provides an interesting comparison with its diminutive, pointy-petalled ancestors from four centuries earlier.

The Dutch Historic collection never stands still, and this is part of its appeal. Each year a few new varieties become available through my sources, emerging as if by magic from decades or centuries past, and I succumb to the temptation of adding them to the mix. Conversely, each year a few varieties do less well despite my best efforts, either being targeted by hungry rodents or simply fading away, the bulbs diminishing in size until they no longer have the strength to bloom. I appreciate every single tulip, from the moment it pushes a shoot up through the cold earth in February through its flowering period to the time when it is lifted in July, all the while accepting that tulips are by their very nature ephemeral.

Dutch Historic broken tulips are displayed in a collection of old
soda bottles, with the modern Rembrandt *Tulipa* 'Inner Wheel' and
T. 'Insulinde' in the foreground. Overleaf: Pots in the twig house contain
some of the more delicate historic tulips, including Duc van Tol varieties.

Breeder Tulips

T. 'ADMIRAL TROMP'

T. 'AESCULAPIUS'

T. 'ALBA REGALIS'

T. 'ARCHERON'

T. 'BLEU AIMABLE'

T. 'COTTAGE MAID'

T. 'DILLENBURG'

T. 'DOM PEDRO'

T. 'GEORGES GRAPPE'

T. 'JE MAINTIENDRAI'

T. 'KEIZERSKROON'

T. 'KLOPSTOCK'

T. 'LA JOYEUSE'

T. 'LAC VAN RIJN'

T. 'LE MOGUL'

T. 'MADRAS'

T. 'MAYFLOWER'

T. 'OLD TIMES'

T. 'QUEEN ALEXANDRA'

T. 'SIMON BOLIVAR'

A BREEDER TULIP is plain or 'self'-coloured, also known at various points through history as a mother tulip. It might have a flush of colour on the midribs or an all-over wash on the exterior of the flower head, but it will always be solid as opposed to patterned with flames or feathers. It is unaffected (or uninfected) by Tulip Breaking Virus (TBV). Breeders are named as such because they were the parent stock from which broken tulips (see p.120) were bred; the name 'mother' arose for the same reason. In early herbals and florilegia they were described as 'self' because they were self-coloured, although the base was nearly always a contrasting shade. During the seventeenth century they were held in less high esteem than their flamed and feathered counterparts, but were nevertheless an important commodity that sold for considerable sums. Today's collectors of historic breeder tulips are intent on keeping them unbroken, in their original state, since they will never wholly revert to breeders once they have broken; my breeder bulbs of 'Klopstock' have nearly all broken, despite my best efforts, and I miss the richness of their pure purple petals.

Breeders have come in and out of fashion at various periods of their long history, reaching a peak during the heyday of florists' societies in the nineteenth century, when tulips were shown in separate classes for breeders and broken forms (as indeed they still are today at the Wakefield and North of England Tulip Society Annual Show). At the end of the nineteenth century the launch of a range of breeders known as Darwin tulips (now incorporated into Division 5, Single Late) precipitated an explosion of garden hybrids intended as bedding tulips. A proliferation of tulips was registered at this period, reflected in the content of our historic collection. Dutch Historic breeders were traditionally categorized into three or more different colourways (see p.151) – Rose (or Rosen/Rozen), Bybloemen (or Violetten) and Bizarre (or Bizarren) – but these have become of less importance today and are generally referred to only in relation to English Florists' tulips (see Chapter 3). Included in this section are a few single or bicoloured tulips that are not perceived as breeders, and these have been noted in the individual profiles.

T. 'ADMIRAL TROMP'

In the nursery catalogue entitled 'Book of Flowering Bulbs' issued by Van Bourgondien Bros in 1939, 'Admiral Tromp' (see opposite, top left) features under the heading 'Breeder Bulbs for the Connoisseur', and is described as 'Bright orange-red, shaded salmon. One of the finest Breeder Tulips recently introduced; large and strong flower. Height 29 inches.' Priced at $2.50 per dozen, it was one of the company's most expensive tulips, and the catalogue entry is graced with a glorious full-colour photograph. I find this cultivar – one of a few surviving Dutch breeder tulips introduced in the early twentieth century in 'Art Shades' of yellows, browns and oranges – a worthy alternative to 'Dillenburg', slightly later to make its appearance, with a larger flower head and attractive base of orange-yellow-tinged khaki. It is named after the Dutch admiral Maarten Tromp (1598–1653), who commanded his country's navy in the First Anglo-Dutch War, or after his second son, Cornelis (1629–1691), who also reached the rank of admiral.

DIVISION: 5 (Single Late)
DATE: Registered by C. G. van Tubergen in 1932
HEIGHT: 60 cm (24 in)
FLOWERING TIME: May

T. 'AESCULAPIUS'

Dark violet brushed over with a shimmer of bronze, the petals have a substantial, fleshy consistency that has proven to be wonderfully weatherproof (see opposite, below left). Inside, a white zigzag base bleeds into a band of blue, which is echoed in the colour of the short, fat stamens. Leaves are wide and undulate, the stem bright lime-green in perfect contrast to the flower colour. This vibrant cultivar breaks readily, but in an unusually subtle fashion, presenting in shades of purple without revealing the white base colour. In Greco-Roman mythology Aesculapius was the son of Apollo and the god of healing and medicine.

DIVISION: 5 (Single Late)
DATE: Registered by Vincent van der Vinne of Haarlem in 1863
HEIGHT: 40 cm (16 in)
FLOWERING TIME: May

T. 'ALBA REGALIS'

This old tulip (how old is hard to say; the most common dates are 1620 and 1670) is small, delicate and scented, with a loosely lily-flowered form (see opposite, top right). Paper-thin petals start out yellowish cream and bleach to pure white, occasionally with a green tip, and are long and narrow; the outer three reflex outwards, while the inner three cup slightly inwards. The inside is completely white, with no contrasting base, the anthers are pale yellow and the stigma white. The slender stem bends to the wind – this trait, which helps to extend the flowering time, has been bred out of many modern tulips to achieve a ramrod-straight appearance. 'Alba Regalis' is almost like a miniature version of 'Très Chic' or the even larger 'White Triumphator'. The Lily-flowered division (Division 6) was created in 1958 to accommodate the new forms that were being bred, but its roots can be seen in this early antique prototype. It should be noted that 'Alba Regalis' is not typically regarded as a breeder tulip, and it has never broken in my custodianship.

DIVISION: 1 (Single Early)
DATE: 1620 (unconfirmed)
HEIGHT: 20–25 cm (8–10 in)
FLOWERING TIME: April

T. 'ARCHERON'

Deep garnet-red with a tinge of rust on the exterior of the three outer petals, the inner three notched and a lighter shade lower down, verging on pink (see opposite, below right). The texture of the petals is lustrously smooth, causing light to bounce off them and making these elegant tulips particularly eye-catching. Inside, the base is inky blue and the stamens deep black, creating a moody feel befitting the name 'Archeron', the river over which, according to Greek mythology, Charon ferried the dead to Hades. The stigma, however, is a contrasting bright white. A tall, slender stem of mid-green has wide basal leaves. This is one of the most richly coloured breeder tulips still available. It was popular in the United States in the 1920s, when it was offered for sale by Maurice Fuld Inc. of New York in its catalogue 'My Garden Favorites. Devoted to a Complete Listing of "Just Delightfully Different" Holland Bulbs for Direct Import'.

DIVISION: 5 (Single Late)
DATE: 1913
HEIGHT: 40 cm (16 in)
FLOWERING TIME: Late April

T. 'BLEU AIMABLE'

This unusual tulip (see opposite, top left) was described as 'Blue-mauve shaded violet, with electric-blue centre, handsome' in Barr & Sons' Gold Medal bulb catalogue in 1936. I find the colouration less definable than this suggests, more of a bruised lilac with darker overtones, the base blue as though brushed on with delicate strokes. It should be noted that there has never been a true blue tulip (or a real black one, for that matter), so the name represents hope over experience. 'Bleu Aimable' is an old Krelage Darwin tulip (that gave rise to the sport 'Blue Parrot'), and it is the first of our twentieth-century Dutch breeders to flower each spring. Variegation on the outside petals fades with age – indeed, the colouring as a whole fades as the flower matures – while the stems are deep lilac at the top, bleeding to green as they meet the grey-green leaves. Stamens are blue. Whether grown in the flower field, massed in a container or harvested as a cut flower, this cultivar has a luminescent quality that makes it stand out.

DIVISION: 5 (Single Late)
DATE: Registered by E. H. Krelage & Son in 1916
HEIGHT: 60 cm (24 in)
FLOWERING TIME: April

T. 'COTTAGE MAID'
Synonym: T. 'La Précieuse'

A charmingly old-fashioned tulip, which looks as though it has come straight out of a cottage garden. Rosy-pink petals come to gentle points, their centres flooded with white on the inside and outside of the flower head; the white continues right to the tips on the outer three petals, stopping halfway up the inner ones (see opposite, below left). A bright yellow base and yellow anthers and filaments complete this pretty picture. It breaks readily, but very attractively (although it is not classed as a breeder by Hortus Bulborum). As a precaution I keep it well away from other breeders in the historic collection, in order that it doesn't infect them with TBV. Very popular in the United States in the first quarter of the twentieth century, 'Cottage Maid' has all but disappeared, ousted by much newer, bolder varieties. 'Flaming Purissima' is perhaps its present-day equivalent, flowering concurrently, similar in colouration but many times the size.

DIVISION: 1 (Single Early)
DATE: 1857
HEIGHT: 25 cm (10 in)
FLOWERING TIME: Early April

T. 'DILLENBURG'

Championed and grown by the plantsman Christopher Lloyd at his famous garden at Great Dixter in East Sussex, where he trickled the bulbs through the borders, 'Dillenburg' is a magnificent tulip that starts flowering in early May and continues for several weeks (see opposite, top right). Described by Lloyd as 'orange', but with a pink flush on the three outside petals, it also shows a tendency to be lightly feathered in pale orange at the edges of the petals. The yellow of the base extends up the central beam; the stigma is pronounced, stems strong and thick, leaves slightly wavy. More sophisticated than it sounds, 'Dillenburg' is another of the cluster of tulips bred for their moody, indefinable 'Art Shades'. The slightly elongated, scented flower heads open wide to the sun, and hold on to their petals obligingly whether growing outside or cut for a vase.

DIVISION: 5 (Single Late)
DATE: Registered by C. G. van Tubergen in 1916
HEIGHT: 65 cm (26 in)
FLOWERING TIME: Early May

T. 'DOM PEDRO'

The first historic tulip I ever bought, 'Dom Pedro' has a lot to answer for, because it kick-started the habit of a lifetime. Large mahogany-brown heads are lightly shaded in bronze at the edges, where they catch the light beguilingly (see opposite, below right). The insides have a reddish tinge on a cadmium-yellow base. Described in the John Lewis Childs bulb catalogue of 1920 as 'undoubtedly the most attractive of the brown tulips', it is another of the few Dutch breeders cultivated in 'Art Shades'. Reintroduced to the mainstream market in 2016, 'Dom Pedro' has become a victim of its own success and is almost impossible to obtain. With long stems and longevity (it was recorded in the Report of the Tulip Nomenclature Committee 1914–15 as being in flower for twenty days), it makes a spectacular cut flower that puts on more growth in the vase than any other historic tulip I grow. It now grows in rough grass at Blacklands, part of the chaotic mix of flowers on the way to the compost bay (see pp.4–5), because I had so many offsets that I had to plant them out after their first season.

DIVISION: 5 (Single Late)
DATE: 1911
HEIGHT: 60 cm (24 in)
FLOWERING TIME: Early May

T. 'GEORGES GRAPPE'

Enormous egg-shaped heads of lavender-blue sit on top of impossibly tall, slender stems (see opposite, top left). The three exterior petals shimmer with a wash of copper, while the interior three have a white midrib, most pronounced on the inside, where it appears as a stripe. A base of smoky blue bleeds into the petal colour, and bright white anthers echo the white lines at the centres of the petals; pollen is heavy and black, and spills across the petals. As the flower ages, the head opens out to a diameter of almost 20 cm (8 in), creating a striking picture. Once cut and placed in water, this extraordinary tulip moves exquisitely, twisting and turning over a period of more than two weeks as it slowly ages and dies. Georges Grappe was a French art critic and writer who was curator of the Musée Rodin in Paris in the early twentieth century and produced biographies of artists, among them Jean Honoré Fragonard.

DIVISION: 5 (Single Late)
DATE: Registered by C. G. van Tubergen in 1939
HEIGHT: 65 cm (26 in)
FLOWERING TIME: May

T. 'JE MAINTIENDRAI'
Synonym: *T.* 'Sentinel'

This tall and exceptionally elegant tulip has petals of amethyst and burnt copper, with a clearly defined lemon-yellow base (see opposite, below left). The flower head is an elegant cup shape, on the small side for the first few years, but the size contributes to its long flowering period, since it can better withstand extremes of weather. It has been thoroughly tested by the worst weather that Wiltshire can throw at it, and endeared itself all the more to me by surviving unscathed. It is frequently – and inaccurately – recorded as having been introduced in 1963. The introduction of the Darwin race of tulips by E. H. Krelage & Son in 1899 challenged the position of more subtle, sinuous tulips, such as this one.

DIVISION: 5 (Single Late)
DATE: Registered by Vincent van der Vinne of Haarlem in 1863
HEIGHT: 60 cm (24 in)
FLOWERING TIME: Late April–early May

T. 'KEIZERSKROON'
Synonym: *T.* 'Grand Duc'

Bright scarlet, globe-shaped flowers are edged with a wide margin of golden yellow, the red coming to a sharp point on the three outer petals but halting about a third of the way up the inner three (see opposite, top right). On the inside of the flower a wide band of red extends all the way round, above a strong yellow base. Anthers are a contrasting black, heavy with pollen. Leaves are grey-green, the three basal ones wide and those higher up the stem more lanceolate. *Keizerskroon* is Dutch for 'imperial crown', and these striking flowers really do look like a simplistic drawing of a crown, decidedly regal in their unapologetically bright colouring. Immensely popular as a bedding tulip in the twentieth century owing to its reliability and robustness, this cultivar has fallen out of fashion, to be replaced with taller tulips in less vibrant shades. However, I enjoy the fact that a tulip more than 270 years old can make such an impact in the early spring garden. Part of the reason for this cultivar's popularity was that it is not prone to breaking (it is not technically a breeder tulip). As its synonym suggests, it is in fact a larger version of 'Duc van Tol Red and Yellow' (see p.134).

DIVISION: 1 (Single Early)
DATE: 1750
HEIGHT: 30–35 cm (12–14 in)
FLOWERING TIME: Early April

T. 'KLOPSTOCK'

An unusually deep bishop's purple, with a clean white base surrounded by a mid-blue corona (see opposite, below right). Opens generously in the sun so that the inner markings can be observed. A satisfyingly even flower head, slightly elongated, sits atop a long, slender stem. Good for picking, 'Klopstock' lasts well in the vase. It reliably produces several offsets each year, performs well in the ground or in a container, and is surprisingly happy in an unheated greenhouse, so long as you remember to water it regularly. Breaks rather too readily (although strikingly), so keep the breeder bulbs well away from broken ones to maintain the integrity of breeder stocks.

DIVISION: 5 (Single Late)
DATE: Registered by Vincent van der Vinne of Haarlem in 1863
HEIGHT: 45 cm (18 in)
FLOWERING TIME: Late April–early May

T. 'LA JOYEUSE'

An ethereal dirty pink, tinged green at the centre of the petals (although not strictly speaking variegated), becoming paler at the edges (see opposite, top left). Variously described as 'silvery-grey flushed with lilac' (Franken Brothers autumn catalogue, 1923) and 'an exquisite, pinky-heliotrope' (by the Rev. Joseph Jacob in *Tulips*, 1912), it is hard to pin down its colour – as is the case with so many of the Dutch Historic breeders. At one time classed as a Cottage tulip, although from its name one would assume it to be French rather than English in origin. This tulip lives up to its name and brings great joy. It has a presence that is difficult to define, but is best described as being imbued with antiquity – even though it is not that old within the Dutch Historic collection. The head is relatively small and supremely elegant; the petals reflex gently outwards in the sun and a white base has a corona of pigment-rich pale inky blue. Long stems and slender leaves are imbued with a burgundy hue and add to the appeal of 'La Joyeuse' as a cut flower.

DIVISION: 5 (Single Late)
DATE: Registered by Vincent van der Vinne of Haarlem in 1863
HEIGHT: 50 cm (20 in)
FLOWERING TIME: Late April–May

T. 'LAC VAN RIJN'

One of the earliest cultivars in the collection, 'Lac van Rijn' is dainty and diminutive with pointy petals of pinkish-purple edged with a wide band of white and a clear yellow base (see opposite, below left). Although 1620 is the general date of attribution, it is likely to have been grown before this, judging by its inclusion in the compositions of Dutch still-life painters of the day (see p.23). Despite its delicacy, 'Lac van Rijn' is a robust little tulip that has stood the test of time, partly because it does not break (and is not strictly a breeder tulip). One carefully picked stem placed in a bud vase will delight for days. The temptation to pick the bottom leaves along with the flower must be avoided, despite the fact that they seem to belong with such a small bloom. They should be left on the plant so that the energy can be reabsorbed into the bulb.

DIVISION: 1 (Single Early)
DATE: 1620
HEIGHT: 25 cm (10 in)
FLOWERING TIME: Early to mid-April

T. 'LE MOGUL'

The Report of the Tulip Nomenclature Committee of 1914–15 records 'Le Mogul' as coming into flower on 8 May and continuing to bloom for eighteen days. It is indeed one of the longest-flowering breeder tulips we grow at Blacklands, standing up to the vagaries of the British weather despite its tall, slender stems. Intense pinkish-mauve petals are overlaid with the faintest bronze wash, and the pure white base has an indigo-blue corona (see opposite, top right). Cup-shaped flowers and neat, lanceolate leaves make this a very tidy tulip to grow. 'Le Mogul' was offered for sale in the E. H. Krelage & Son bulb catalogue of 1916 under the heading 'Dutch Breeder Tulips', and featured in a display of breeder and Darwin tulips at the New York Botanical Garden in 1921. It has kept a low profile ever since.

DIVISION: 5 (Single Late)
DATE: 1913
HEIGHT: 60 cm (24 in)
FLOWERING TIME: May

T. 'MADRAS'

The flower head is an alluring deep bronze with lighter flecks, goblet-shaped and elegant (see opposite, below right). We used this liberally in garden containers for several seasons since it was readily available through mainstream bulb catalogues and reasonably priced. At the end of each season we lifted it, dried the bulbs, then planted them in the wild banks at the back of the house. Little did we realize that 'Madras' would suddenly disappear completely from the bulb catalogues and become almost impossible to obtain. We now enjoy its annual appearance in a riotous medley along the edge of the drive, where it brings a touch of reverence and sophistication to the dolly-mixture effect of recycled container bulbs. I await its return commercially, when I will purchase some new bulbs from which I can propagate bulblets and build up my own stock.

DIVISION: 5 (Single Late)
DATE: 1913
HEIGHT: 60 cm (24 in)
FLOWERING TIME: May

T. 'MAYFLOWER'

Light scarlet heads of considerable size are an elongated claret-glass shape, the petals slightly wavy at the edges (see opposite, top left). In infancy the exteriors are flushed with khaki, but this fades as the flower matures. On a sunny day the petals open to a width of over 20 cm (8 in), revealing segments of pale indigo blue at the base of each petal, each wedge shape feathered all the way round with white. It has an extremely attractive interior that presses beautifully. Purple anthers more than 1 cm (⅓ in) long and very thin rise vertically out of the filaments. The stems are slender, making the tulip look top-heavy, but it has no problem staying upright. Leaves are narrow, tending to lime-green. 'Mayflower' is a prolific tulip, producing a good tally of offsets. Its petals do not mark in foul weather, retaining their colour and form throughout the long flowering period. Be aware that it is prone to breaking readily; my breeder stocks are much diminished, having mostly broken over the years.

DIVISION: 5 (Single Late)
DATE: Registered by C. G. van Tubergen in 1922
HEIGHT: 45 cm (18 in)
FLOWERING TIME: Late April–May

T. 'OLD TIMES'

A personal favourite, 'Old Times' is another early twentieth-century breeder tulip sold under the heading 'Art Shades'. An old Cottage tulip, it is relatively short-stemmed in comparison with its unusually long, narrow flower heads. A ground of egg-yolk yellow is overlaid with a deep rusty pinkish purple, both inside and out, the colour more intense up the central rib (see opposite, below left). The flower heads never open fully; instead, the petals reflex gently as they age, their slightly pointed tips turning pleasingly outwards as the colours soften and fade. This is a breeder tulip that breaks readily, so it is critical the breeder bulbs are kept separate from broken ones. That said, when it does break it does so elegantly, with symmetrical feathering at the edges of the petals. Although 'Old Times' is recorded as being registered in 1919, it may be older, since the Rev. Joseph Jacob wrote in 1912 of rescuing it from a garden in Flintshire 'where it had been growing for between fifty and sixty years'.

DIVISION: 5 (Single Late)
DATE: 1919
HEIGHT: 50 cm (20 in)
FLOWERING TIME: May

T. 'QUEEN ALEXANDRA'

This is an unusually tall breeder tulip with generously sized flower heads of a lemon-yellow ground colour, overlaid with a rich pinkish-brown (see opposite, top right). The petals come to a slight point and curve gently inwards. Beautiful in containers and excellent as a cut flower, it is rather wasted in the flower field, and I plan to grow it in pots to enjoy in the garden. Produces a good quantity of bulblets, so I don't have to be too precious about cutting from it, as long as the lower leaves are left so that they can help the bulb build up energy stores. Barr & Sons offered 'Queen Alexandra' for sale in its bulb catalogue in 1936, describing it as 'very robust, height 3 ft [91 cm]' – mine have not reached those heights yet.

DIVISION: 5 (Single Late)
DATE: Registered by Barr & Sons in c.1900
HEIGHT: 60 cm (24 in)
FLOWERING TIME: May

T. 'SIMON BOLIVAR'

In the Dutch tradition of naming tulips after military leaders, this joyous Single Late variety was registered in the name of the Venezuelan soldier and statesman Simón Bolívar, 'El Libertador' (The Liberator), who freed much of South America from Spanish rule between 1819 and 1825. This tulip is a bright peachy-orange, flushed yellow at the edges, with a yellow base (see opposite, below right). The petals are elongated and nicely rounded at their tips. Leaves are disproportionately large in relation to the rest of the flower, lending a somewhat scruffy appearance to an otherwise attractive cultivar. For this reason I use it as a cut flower; arranged with browns and purples, it shines. Late to flower in our collection, this is a reliable, weatherproof tulip that produces good-sized offsets that flower with small blooms in their first year (it is more usual for an offset to take two or three years to reach flowering size).

DIVISION: 5 (Single Late)
DATE: Registered by J. J. Grullemans & Sons in 1944
HEIGHT: 60 cm (24 in)
FLOWERING TIME: May

Broken Tulips

T. 'ABSALON'

T. 'BLACK AND WHITE'

T. 'BRIDESMAID'

T. 'INNER WHEEL'

T. 'INSULINDE'

T. 'THE LIZARD'

T. 'REMBRANDTTULP'

T. 'RUBELLA'

T. 'RUBENS'

T. 'SASKIA'

T. 'SILVER STANDARD'

T. 'STRIPED SAIL'

A TRUE BROKEN tulip has been infected by Tulip Breaking Virus (TBV), causing the outer layer of colour (anthocyanin) to break up into patterns, revealing the base colour of white or yellow. Most – but, confusingly, not all – broken tulips are placed in the Rembrandt division (Division 9). *Tulipa* 'Silver Standard', for instance, is classed as a Single Early (and it does flower considerably earlier than the rest of the broken Dutch Historic tulips in our collection at Blacklands). Broken tulips are also referred to as 'rectified' and 'variegated', or, if you want to be more prosaic, 'striped'. There is a rich lexicon used to describe the markings themselves, starting with 'flamed' (an intensification of the top layer of colour up the midrib and around the edges) and 'feathered' (a concentration of markings on the petal edges, as opposed to the centre). In the past they have also been referred to as jaspis, marbled, jagged, striated and stippled, according to the type of marking.

Such definitions are rarely used to describe Dutch Historic tulips today because the patterns on their petals have been allowed to randomize and become irregular. Perfect symmetry was highly prized during the seventeenth century, as is evident in the tulips that feature in the paintings of the Dutch Golden Age, although definition of colour was perhaps rated even more highly. Most broken tulips are no longer selectively bred to produce concise markings. I enter our Dutch Historic tulips into the Vase Classes at the Wakefield and North of England Tulip Society Annual Show, and they are judged on how they conform to type, their uniformity and how well grown they are; regularity of markings does not count – unlike with English Florists' tulips (see Chapter 3), where perfectly marked flames and feathers are key to success on the showbench. The overlying contrasting colour of a broken tulip will be significantly deeper in shade than its breeder counterpart, often making it hard to identify which cultivar a rogue break has come from.

T. 'ABSALON'

This striking egg-shaped tulip has flames and feathers of rich mahogany over a primrose-yellow base, the contrasting colours being immensely pleasing (see opposite, top left). It has a habit of trying to revert to the rich brown colour of the breeder over successive seasons, leaving little of the yellow except for a couple of splashes on the petals. This is an unusual characteristic for a historic tulip; the risk is generally of a breeder breaking to broken form, rather than the opposite. 'Absalon' is robust and quick to propagate, and does not seem to have been weakened by TBV. It has survived in significant numbers for about 250 years and is one of the few old broken varieties to be consistently available for purchase today. Theories abound as to whether the virus is still present but in a weaker form, or whether the plant has become genetically stable since its original infection and is no longer diseased. Either way, it is said that 'Absalon' can be grown near breeder bulbs without fear, although I still can't quite bring myself to do that, and for now I keep it in the broken section of our growing field.

DIVISION: 9 (Rembrandt)
DATE: 1780
HEIGHT: 50 cm (20 in)
FLOWERING TIME: Late April–early May

T. 'BLACK AND WHITE'

This is a brand-new hybrid, recently discovered at Hortus Bulborum in Limmen, the Netherlands, and as yet unregistered with KAVB (see opposite, below left). I grew it for the first time in 2022, having obtained a few bulbs. It is not really black and white, for no tulip is truly black; rather, it is varying shades of dark burgundy on a creamy background, not entirely dissimilar to 'Rembrandttulp' but with less flamboyant markings and a significantly smaller flower head. This tulip dies as beautifully as it lives, opening its petals completely to reveal the inner markings, while holding on to them for several days in a state of suspended grace.

DIVISION: 9 (Rembrandt)
DATE: Early twentieth century
HEIGHT: 40 cm (16 in)
FLOWERING TIME: May

T. 'BRIDESMAID'
Synonym: T. 'Maid of Honour'

'Rather long flower with pointed petals, cherry crimson broadly flamed white, centre peacock blue, very attractive', according to Barr & Sons' Gold Medal bulb catalogue of 1936. 'Bridesmaid' is a short, late-flowering tulip with clear markings, more distinct on the inside of the flower than the outside (see opposite, top right), which works well with its habit of opening right out to the sun. A distinctive blue base adds to the general appeal. Slender, wavy stems make it less vulnerable to wind damage, aided perhaps by the fact that it comes into bloom late in the spring. Petals frequently number five or seven rather than the standard six, and are narrow at the base with gaps between them (known as quartering), most evident when the flower is fully blown. 'Bridesmaid' is fecund despite its small stature, producing many offsets, which flower within a year or two.

DIVISION: 9 (Rembrandt)
DATE: Registered by E. H. Krelage & Son in 1900
HEIGHT: 30–35 cm (12–14 in)
FLOWERING TIME: May

T. 'INNER WHEEL'

'Inner Wheel' is a modern Rembrandt type bred in the vein of an old broken tulip, and as such poses no risk of TBV infection to other stock. With flames of deep raspberry and the palest purple on a white background (see opposite, below right), it appears more antique than its date would suggest, although comparisons with the slightly similar 'Insulinde' highlight the fact that, while 'Inner Wheel' has a considerably larger flower head and longer stem, its markings are less refined. A bright white base is bordered with inky blue that extends up the central beam of the petals on the inside, making this impressive tulip as attractive when open to the sun as it is when closed.

DIVISION: 9 (Rembrandt)
DATE: 2008
HEIGHT: 60 cm (24 in)
FLOWERING TIME: May

T. 'INSULINDE'

One of the most beautiful Dutch Historic tulips, with painterly swirls of raspberry and mauve wrapped around creamy white petals, and the odd, random splash of yellow (see opposite, top left). No two flowers are the same, and when they are massed in a bed, container or vase, the effect is mesmerizing. A hint of blue extends from the base of the petals, and the bright yellow stigma is prominent. Leaves are large and unruly, which should be borne in mind if planting in a container since they do not make a pretty picture. The flower heads are goblet-shaped and attractive from bud to dying days, making this an excellent cut flower. If you have ambitions to show your tulips, 'Insulinde' is a good option for Vase Classes 1 and 2 (for Dutch tulips not English Florists' tulips) at the Wakefield and North of England Tulip Society Annual Show and makes a good talking point. One of a handful of old broken varieties that are considered to be genetically stable, 'Insulinde' is offered by an increasing number of wholesalers. Invest in as many bulbs as you can justify.

DIVISION: 9 (Rembrandt)
DATE: Registered by E. H. Krelage & Son c.1915
HEIGHT: 45 cm (18 in)
FLOWERING TIME: Late April–early May

T. 'THE LIZARD'

The large flower heads of this tulip are indeed shaped somewhat like a lizard's head, elongated and often inclining slightly to one side (see opposite, below left). If you find yourself looking at a bed of this mesmerizing Rembrandt, as I have done at Hortus Bulborum in the Netherlands, you will see what I mean. Flames of bright raspberry-pink and red are broken by streaks of vibrant lemon-yellow, with the odd white flash. Inside, the yellow is more dominant, with an undefined yellow base blending up into the petals – although the tulip never opens out fully to the sun to reveal the beauty within. Leaves are glaucous and faintly streaked with a light burgundy. The cultivar was described in the catalogue of the American breeder John Scheepers & Co. in 1919 as 'Large flower on graceful stem; of unusual markings'.

DIVISION: 9 (Rembrandt)
DATE: 1903
HEIGHT: 45 cm (18 in)
FLOWERING TIME: May

T. 'REMBRANDTTULP'

Tall and painterly with defined flames of purple-burgundy on pale to intense yellow (see opposite, top right). Similar to 'Insulinde' but with a longer stem, the splashes of colour a little less mauve and more yellow. A bright yellow base runs straight into the yellow of the petals; the stigma is yellow and anthers deep black. The top of the stem is stained dark burgundy, bleeding down into a clean green. This is a contentious tulip because its origins are unclear. Usually that is perceived as a good thing with a historic tulip since it proves that its antiquity pre-dates modern record-keeping, but 'Rembrandttulp' is not old enough to qualify for that. The KAVB Classified List of Tulips (1996) records a scarlet tulip named 'Rembrandt' dating to before 1900, and the E. H. Krelage & Son bulb catalogue of 1916 offers for sale a Single Early 'Rembrandt' of scarlet with a yellow base. There is no record of a broken one, but my assumption is that the examples we have at Blacklands are breaks from this parent.

DIVISION: 9 (Rembrandt)
DATE: 1915
HEIGHT: 50 cm (20 in)
FLOWERING TIME: Late April–May

T. 'RUBELLA'

Pale yellow ground overlaid with streaks of bright red, raspberry-pink and cream, the markings spread evenly over the whole flower head (see opposite, below right). The yellow fades to white as the flower ages. White base, with a dash of indigo at the bottom of each petal and matching dark indigo stamens. A quiet tulip, less striking than most others in our collection, but so far proving reliable and robust. I have been growing it for only a few seasons, so time will tell whether it is happy with us in Wiltshire. The stems are strong with good height, the leaves a bright lime-green. *Rubella* is Latin for 'little red', and is used repeatedly to describe tulips in Matthias de L'Obel's *Plantarum seu stirpium historia* of 1576.

DIVISION: 9 (Rembrandt)
DATE: Early twentieth century
HEIGHT: 45 cm (18 in)
FLOWERING TIME: May

T. 'RUBENS'

One of the last of our broken Dutch Historic tulips to flower, 'Rubens' is also one of the most striking. Smallish goblet-shaped heads are heavily marked with bright cerise over an egg-yolk-yellow background, creating a 'splintered' effect across the petals (see opposite, top left). The distribution of pattern is surprisingly symmetrical for a Dutch Historic tulip, most obviously so on the inside, where the yellow of the base extends upwards in attractive stripes. Petals are irregular at the edges, so in its final days, when fully blown to the sun, 'Rubens' can resemble a flamboyant parrot tulip, albeit a rather small one.

DIVISION: 9 (Rembrandt)
DATE: Early twentieth century
HEIGHT: 45 cm (18 in)
FLOWERING TIME: May

T. 'SASKIA'

'Saskia' is a striking tulip of strong yellow with regal red flames and feathers, the yellow ground colour fading completely to ivory over time (see opposite, below left). The flower head is square in profile at its base, with wavy edged petals prone to reflexing at their rounded tips. Anthers produce heavy black pollen, which can be gently blown away or removed with a damp paintbrush should you wish to display a perfect specimen in a vase or as a still-life subject. Stems are delicate, and the leaves – always three in number – undulate gently, echoing the shape of the petals. Markings very variable, some pleasingly symmetrical, others heavily blocked in red or yellow; I destroy all but the best examples, to maintain the quality of stock from which I propagate. The Dutch painter Rembrandt's wife and muse, Saskia, was the model for his painting of Flora, Roman goddess of flowers and fertility, that hangs in the State Hermitage Museum, St Petersburg. Executed in 1634 (the year of the couple's marriage), this portrait is the first and most famous of the artist's three renditions of Flora, with a sizeable red-and-white rectified tulip placed prominently at the side of her headdress.

DIVISION: 9 (Rembrandt)
DATE: Registered by T. Storer in 1958
HEIGHT: 30–35 cm (12–14 in)
FLOWERING TIME: Late April–May

T. 'SILVER STANDARD'

The flower head is of a loose form, bulbous at the base, the petals gently tapering to a point (see opposite, top right). Variable random markings, some examples heavily flamed, others much lighter. The proportions are not perfect, with the stem quite short for the size of the flower head. This is the earliest of our historic tulips to flower, and its stark red-and-white blooms stand out graphically within the raised beds at the start of spring (see pp.98–99). Of all the historic tulips I grow, this is the most evocative of the now extinct crimson-and-white 'Semper Augustus' (see p.96), the tulip that is synonymous with Tulipmania in seventeenth-century Holland.

DIVISION: 1 (Single Early)
DATE: 1760
HEIGHT: 35 cm (14 in)
FLOWERING TIME: April

T. 'STRIPED SAIL'

This is possibly my least favourite tulip in the Dutch Historic collection, yet ironically it is the most prolific. It produces many offsets each year, all a good size, in a blatant bid to consume ever more of my growing space. Suffice to say that many are given away or composted, to prevent a total takeover. Its markings are best described as chunky, consisting of jagged blocks of purple-red on a bright yellow base that are slightly jarring, rather than exciting the eye (see opposite, below right). That said, over the few weeks that it flowers (for it is long-flowering) the yellow mellows slowly to white and the red becomes pinker, rendering the blooms easier to tolerate and quite effective when massed in a vase. 'Striped Sail' – a sport of 'White Sail' (c.1915) – is not a true broken tulip but a bicoloured Triumph in the vein of an old Mendel type.

DIVISION: 3 (Triumph)
DATE: Registered by T. Bakker Mz in 1960
HEIGHT: 40 cm (16 in)
FLOWERING TIME: April

Duc van Tol

T. 'DUC VAN TOL COCHINEAL'

T. 'DUC VAN TOL MAX CRAMOISIE'

T. 'DUC VAN TOL PRIMROSE'

T. 'DUC VAN TOL RED AND WHITE'

T. 'DUC VAN TOL RED AND YELLOW'

T. 'DUC VAN TOL SALMON'

T. 'DUC VAN TOL SCARLET'

THE DUC VAN TOL RACE OF TULIPS (also called Duc van Thols, Dukes and Ducs) are often mistaken for species (botanical) tulips because of their dwarf scale and early flowering (pictured opposite is 'Duc van Tol Primrose' on the left, 'Duc van Tol Red and White' in the centre and 'Duc van Tol Cochineal' on the right). While they are descended from the wild *Tulipa schrenkii* (syn. *T. suaveolens*), they are in fact annual (garden) tulips with a long history of cultivation dating back more than 400 years: *T.* 'Duc van Tol Red and Yellow' (c.1595) is the earliest tulip at the Hortus Bulborum and in our Dutch Historic collection at Blacklands. John Parkinson referred to these tulips in his *Paradisi in Sole Paradisus Terrestris* (1629). Out of a total of about seventeen different Duc van Tol cultivars that have been registered over the centuries,

we currently hold a group of eight, planted in rows in the flower field and in terracotta pots in the walled garden. Flowering begins in mid-March, but they lend themselves to forcing and can be brought into flower for Christmas with the right techniques. The catalogue issued in 1920 by the US bulb distributor John Lewis Childs sings their praises: 'these are the best of all for house culture and the first of all to bloom out of doors. They are noted for the depth and purity of their colours, and as they bloom two weeks in advance of all other Tulips, are quite indispensable in the garden, as well as the house for winter.' At the height of fashion until the 1940s both in the garden and as a cut flower, they are now rarely seen, but are worth growing for the intensity of colour they offer so early in the year.

T. 'DUC VAN TOL COCHINEAL'

This perfect little tulip wins top prize out of all the Duc van Tols I grow, for its colour, form and longevity (see opposite, top left). Bright scarlet petals are glossy in tone and slender in shape, tapering to a point and gently reflexing as the flower comes to the end of its life (a habit that distinguishes it from 'Duc van Tol Scarlet', which is similar in appearance). The yellow base presents in strong contrast to the cochineal-red of the petals, extending about a quarter of the way up the inside of the petal and coming to a slight point at the centre. Stems are strong and upright, with four leaves, the basal one very wide. I dot pots of this bright, early variety around the walled garden to lift the spirits. It copes with the variable spring weather, even standing up to violent hailstorms.

DIVISION: 1 (Single Early)
DATE: 1700
HEIGHT: 25 cm (10 in)
FLOWERING TIME: Late March

T. 'DUC VAN TOL MAX CRAMOISIE'

A beautifully shaped, neat miniature tulip of bright scarlet with a jagged yellow base and jet-black anthers (see opposite, below left). The leaves are wide and glaucous and make a most attractive backdrop for the flowers. Stems are slender and have a tendency to bend under the weight of the flower; for this reason, I tend to grow this variety in pots, where I can give them twiggy supports as needed. The red of the flower works well against terracotta, although I have also tried it in blue-and-white Delftware, a wonderfully arresting combination.

DIVISION: 1 (Single Early)
DATE: 1700
HEIGHT: 25 cm (10 in)
FLOWERING TIME: Early April

T. 'DUC VAN TOL PRIMROSE'

More citrus than primrose (although it flowers concurrently with its namesake), this joyful yellow tulip is self-coloured: yellow all over, with no contrasting base (see opposite, top right). When in bud the outer petals are shaded with green, which fades as it comes into flower, leaving just a slight tinge. It is more cup-shaped than many Duc van Tols, although the petals still come to a slight point. Stamens are pronounced, with large, bright yellow anthers. In contrast, the stigma is small and neat, and very sticky. Leaves generally number three, with a single wide basal one. This is a cheering, hardy little tulip that copes well with poor weather.

DIVISION: 1 (Single Early)
DATE: 1921
HEIGHT: 25 cm (10 in)
FLOWERING TIME: Late March

T. 'DUC VAN TOL RED AND WHITE'

More of a cerise-pink than red, the incurving petals are feathered with painterly white borders and white midribs on the insides (see opposite, below right). The white of the petals starts with a yellow tinge, but this fades after a day or two of sunshine. The yellow base is surprising, since one would normally expect it to be white in a flower of this red-and-white colouration. The stigma is prominent, the anthers purplish and heavy with pollen. Flower heads are diminutive in their first season, becoming increasingly generous in size over successive years but remaining smaller than those of most other Duc van Tols. Opening wide to the sun, they create an attractive star shape.

DIVISION: 1 (Single Early)
DATE: 1805
HEIGHT: 20 cm (8 in)
FLOWERING TIME: Late March

T. 'DUC VAN TOL RED AND YELLOW'

This is the oldest tulip in our Dutch Historic collection, and the first to flower; in fact, it is the first of all our domesticated tulips to bloom (see opposite, centre left). It makes a dramatic appearance in mid-March, its candy colours bursting incongruously out of the bare earth before most of the other tulips are even in bud. Diminutive in stature, it seems almost to flower out of the ground when first in colour (particularly so in a dry spring), the slender stems increasing in length over its brief season. The flower head remains disproportionately large in relation to the stem, even when it reaches its full height. What it lacks in stature, it makes up for in colour with ultra-glossy bright red petals edged with a feathered band of yellow, and a matching yellow base. Moderately wide leaves grow from the foot of the stem in an attractive whorl. The petals are sharply pointed at their tips, reminiscent of the tulips depicted in the Iznik ware of sixteenth-century Turkey. This relic could come straight out of a sultan's prized display in an Ottoman paradise garden.

DIVISION: 1 (Single Early)
DATE: c.1595
HEIGHT: 20 cm (8 in)
FLOWERING TIME: Mid-March

T. 'DUC VAN TOL SALMON'

It is a puzzle why this tulip – almost identical in appearance to 'Duc van Tol Red and Yellow' but bred more than 300 years later (see opposite, far left and centre right) – was introduced on to the commercial market. I can only assume that E. H. Krelage & Son, the famous Dutch nursery, wanted to have a go at creating its own Duc van Tol cultivar to take its place in this illustrious line-up of tulips. Although named 'Salmon' and described as such in the few publications that mention it, it is in fact more of a coral-red with a yellow margin, its head smaller than that of its ancestor and slightly rounder in profile. The petals are less pointed, a sure way to tell it apart from 'Red and Yellow', and the stems slightly longer and slimmer.

DIVISION: 1 (Single Early)
DATE: Registered by E. H. Krelage & Son in 1914
HEIGHT: 25 cm (10 in)
FLOWERING TIME: Mid-March

T. 'DUC VAN TOL SCARLET'

I have never grown another tulip with the same intensity of red as that exhibited by this tiny cultivar dating from the mid-nineteenth century (see opposite, far right); it even beats 'Duc van Tol Red and Yellow'. A dull matt finish to the petals increases the density of colour and renders this variety more easily identifiable, for it is close in appearance to 'Duc van Tol Cochineal'. The flower head is gently goblet-shaped with petals that finish in a sharp needle point. This arresting historic tulip has good powers of endurance when grown outside, helped in part by its sturdy stem and low stature. It holds its own in the flower field, huddled out of the way of the wind, but is in no way shy or retiring.

DIVISION: 1 (Single Early)
DATE: Registered by W. J. Eldering & Son in 1850
HEIGHT: 25 cm (10 in)
FLOWERING TIME: Mid–late March

Clockwise from top left: *Tulipa* 'Striped Sail' planted in a raised bed, with one of the protective structures behind; pots with historic tulips stored behind the cold frames to protect them from the weather; once planted, the historic tulips are labelled individually using black slate markers to avoid any mix-ups of the bulbs; dating from the mid-nineteenth century, 'Duc van Tol Scarlet', with its characteristically short stems, flowers in early spring.

Growing Dutch Historic Tulips

The key to the successful preservation of historic breeder and broken varieties lies in the way in which they are looked after. Whether of more recent breeding or hailing from the time of Tulipmania, every bulb in our Dutch Historic collection is treated in a similar way, with the same tender care lavished upon it. Maintaining a collection of historic bulbs is not for the lazy gardener, and the time necessary for tending these plants and keeping records should not be underestimated.

Planting of the Dutch Historic tulips begins in the second week of November and continues until mid-December, such is the quantity of bulbs that we are dealing with – currently around 2,500. As with all tulips, the timing is important, because the bulbs need a period of cold to kick-start growth (see Vernalization, p.254). The pace of planting is slow, since every process is carried out by hand and must be completed meticulously.

We grow most of the historic bulbs in open ground in the flower field, but a representative quantity is also grown in terracotta containers dotted around the walled garden. The containers serve as back-up stock in case there is an outbreak of tulip fire or stem and bulb nematode in the field beds, and they also provide visual and educational interest in the garden for open days and workshops. When planting, use crocks at the bottom of your pot to ensure good drainage, part fill with the soil mix (see p.246) and position bulbs about 10 cm (4 in) deep. Backfill with the remaining soil mix and top dress smaller pots with a layer of horticultural grit, before covering the containers with protective chicken wire hats (see also p.209). Once planted, we tend to leave them out in the open, rather than under cover, remembering to water them during prolonged dry periods. We grow a single variety in each pot, so that the bulbs don't get mixed up, but the pots can be grouped to create different combinations. It is interesting to place tulips from different periods in pots alongside each other. For instance, 'Alba Regalis', from our historic collection, and 'White Triumphator' (1942), a popular twentieth-century equivalent, are both pure white and lily-flowered, the former almost impossible to obtain, the latter readily available. 'Alba Regalis' is small and neat with

a self-effacing air, while 'White Triumphator' commands attention with its long stems and exaggerated, goblet-shaped flowers. The evolution of tulip-breeding is clearly demonstrated through this comparison, and it is easy to see how 'White Triumphator' won its place in today's garden, but also why 'Alba Regalis' is worth protecting. The only rule when juxtaposing pots is always to keep broken flowers away from breeders to reduce the risk of infection with TBV.

In the flower field we follow a four-year rotation for all our historic tulips, since this is the minimum period recommended to prevent the survival of tulip-fire spores in soil. In an ideal world each bed would lie fallow of tulips for seven years, but this is not always practical. Tulip fire, which can proliferate in warm, damp weather, has the potential to destroy a collection, so we are constantly alert to the signs: spotted and mouldy leaves and flowers. I carefully tear off any foliage that I suspect of being infected, and resort to removing and burning whole plants as necessary. I have sent off samples to the RHS laboratories to be checked, and this is a service I recommend.

In the three years that the beds lie free of tulips, we plant a variety of vegetables and green manures, the likes of mustard caliente, which cleanse the soil and keep it alive with microbial action. We used to cover empty beds with woven polypropylene sheeting to keep them free of weeds, but we soon learned that this was a waste of valuable growing space (not to mention plastic) and seemed to encourage voles to burrow under the improvised shelter – and to return for added snacks when the beds were planted with tulips once more. By keeping the beds constantly filled with plants, we can produce a diverse range of edible and ornamental crops while keeping the surface covered to prevent soil erosion and weed growth. Perhaps most importantly of all, the simple act of sowing plants instead of leaving bare soil has a wider beneficial environmental impact by sequestering carbon.

Tulips are planted in the beds according to size and type. Smaller varieties, such as 'Lac van Rijn' and 'Alba Regalis', are placed in blocks next to each other so that they aren't overshadowed by taller ones. The very early Duc van Tols and Peony types also have their own sections, and the Rembrandt varieties, such as 'Insulinde' and 'Absalon', sit happily alongside each other, their painterly colours and patterns blending throughout the beds. We do plant the historic tulips with colour combinations in mind, preferring either a subtle ombre effect or a vibrant colour clash, rather than an unconsidered medley.

The broken tulips are planted in beds at a distance from the breeder beds to decrease the chance of aphids flying from one to another and spreading TBV. If space doesn't allow us to leave a good distance between breeder and broken beds, we erect vertical barriers of fine mesh to thwart the insects. However many precautions are put in place, there will inevitably be some breaking, and we have to decide whether to destroy or enjoy those infected bulbs. If I wish to keep them because the new markings are of a decent standard, I mark each infected stem with a coloured thread, and the bulb is separated into the broken trays at the time of lifting. Substandard breaks – those with heavy colouration and indistinct, blurred markings – are dug up at the time of flowering and destroyed in order to maintain the overall quality of the collection.

Before planting, the historic tulip beds are excavated to a depth of approximately 20 cm (8 in), and a layer of clean horticultural sand 5 cm (2 in) deep is laid on the newly dug surface. Some specialist growers plant straight on to bare soil, but we have found that a bed of sand improves drainage and prevents the bulbs from rotting. The sand is raked level and the tulips placed seven or nine to a row, depending on the size of the bulb. Smaller bulbs generally result in smaller plants, which need less room than their bulkier counterparts. I plant historic bulbs a little further apart than annuals (see p.217), for the best air circulation and to prevent the foliage from touching. Where quantities of a variety are low (fewer than a dozen, as a rule), the bulbs are planted in plastic vegetable trays placed on top of the sand so that they are easy to locate when the time comes to lift them. I am often to be found at farm shops or restaurants begging for spare plastic trays, which – once

thoroughly cleaned – are lined with a thin layer of sand before the bulbs are planted.

We leave 20 cm (8 in) of fallow soil between the historic varieties so that the different bulbs are kept entirely separate. A tulip bulb can migrate a considerable distance underground, and all bulbs look surprisingly similar when caked in soil. While an accidental mix-up of bulbs wouldn't matter in an annual crop (since the bulbs wouldn't usually be grown again), it is regrettable when historic cultivars get muddled, and it causes havoc with our annual stocktake. I would love to say that this type of accident never happens, but we do have one or two mixes labelled 'Mystery Tulips' until they can be identified at flowering time. The entire collection is catalogued annually for the Plant Heritage National Collection database, and accuracy matters. Each variety is labelled on black markers with the name of the tulip, the year it was first registered and the quantity of bulbs planted.

In addition to keeping the collection well organized, gaps between varieties serve as an effective method of limiting the spread of disease in an organic system, where chemicals cannot be resorted to. There is improved air circulation, which increases the vitality of the plants, and any variety that shows symptoms of a botrytis (including the dreaded tulip fire) can be removed easily, with less risk of contaminating its neighbours. It is important to plant new bulbs separately in a quarantine bed for their first season, to make sure that they don't introduce diseases and put the rest of the collection at risk. Stem and bulb nematode (also known as eelworm), which causes distorted growth, reared its head at Blacklands in 2022, when it arrived in our flower field with some particularly rare bulbs. Because of our organic practices we couldn't use chemical treatment, but the quarantine system and widely spaced planting worked and we were able to extricate the hideously contorted flowers with minimal impact to the larger collection. The bed was left to lie fallow for the next three years.

Once the historic tulips are all in place and labelled, the beds are carefully backfilled. There is generally no need

All the historic tulips are planted on a layer of fine horticultural
sand in individual trays, to keep each variety separate and to help
prevent the spread of disease. Overleaf: *Tulipa* 'Inner Wheel', 'Insulinde'
and 'Rembrandttulp' in flower in the raised beds.

Once lifted, the historic bulbs are cleaned, catalogued, labelled
and sorted into trays before being taken down to the yard for storage.

to water them in after planting, and irrigation of the field tulips is necessary only during a very dry spring. In recent years we have experienced longer periods without rainfall and I have had to water the historic tulip beds once or twice, something I fear will become more regular as a result of climate change. Containers, on the other hand, are checked frequently and watered as required since they dry out more quickly than open soil. We feed the tulips with a dilute organic seaweed formula, once a week when in full growth and once after flowering to aid the production of the new mother bulb. After the second feed they are not watered again, since they should be left to bake in the heat of the sun until lifting time. This is the dream rather than the reality in Wiltshire, but the bulbs are coping so far.

When picking a historic tulip for use as a cut flower, it is important to avoid taking the leaves at the base of the stem since these will continue to photosynthesize and provide energy for the formation of next year's bulbs. The tulips that aren't harvested should be deadheaded after flowering so that they don't put their energy into forming seed, then left until the foliage has withered but the stems are still visible. The stems act as handy markers come harvest time. One year I made the mistake of leaving the bulbs in the ground until August, by which time everything above ground had disappeared and it was almost impossible to locate the bulbs underground. We now make a point of harvesting bulbs by the middle of July, choosing a dry spell so that the bulbs stay clean and to reduce the transferral of mud to labels.

During the whole growing process it is vitally important to handle breeder bulbs and flowers before touching broken ones, to prevent the transfer of TBV. This rule follows right through to the lifting process, when all breeder bulbs are excavated first and stored separately, in much the same way that they are grown. The storage trays are placed on racks with slatted wooden shelves, under cover but outside so that air can circulate but the bulbs remain protected from the elements. Each tray is marked clearly with the variety and quantity of bulb, and the labels from the field beds are placed in the tray with the corresponding tulips. An unfortunate fact of tulip cultivation is that squirrels, rats and mice are drawn to historic bulbs with zero respect for their antiquity or value, so we place inverted empty crates over the full ones and cover them all with mesh to prevent raids.

The Dutch Historic bulbs then lie in stasis until it is time to plant them again. At the beginning of November each bulb is cleaned by hand to remove any remaining soil, and the bulblets peeled away from the mother bulb. Depending on the variety, the brown papery tunic of each bulb is peeled away or left in situ; on some bulbs it falls away and asks to be removed, while with others it clings tightly and is best left intact to protect the white flesh beneath. The cycle is ready to start all over again.

III

English Florists' Tulips

An English Florists' tulip is distinctive in appearance, ideally of a near hemispherical shape, and it must conform to a stringent set of criteria in terms of its petal formations, colours and markings to be exhibited successfully. It is quite different in appearance from most of the Dutch Historic tulips, although cultivars from the two groups grow happily alongside one another to form our National Collection of historic tulips at Blacklands. The English Florists' tulips are a smaller part of the collection in terms of volume – I have amassed dozens of cultivars, some of which are represented by a single bulb – but they are a passion to which I devote an inordinate amount of time and attention.

The name English Florists' is applied to this rarefied family of tulips by dint of the fact that they were bred in England from the beginning of the nineteenth century, as a pastime, by working men who were focused on growing flowers to the highest possible standard and competing against one another at flower shows. Today the word 'florist' denotes a high-street shop selling cut flowers and pot plants, or a professional flower arranger who might decorate a wedding or other event, but until the 1870s the term was applied to specialist growers – whether pure amateurs, gardeners or nurserymen – whose passion it was to produce perfect specimens of a small palette of flowers. The sole focus of the florist was the aesthetic appearance of the flower, with no regard to any other properties or purposes it might have. Its utility was irrelevant, and any religious significance, medicinal or nutritional values it might possess were subjugated entirely to its decorative qualities and how closely they corresponded to the strict set of rules that evolved for each family of flowers.

The word 'florist' came into the lexicon at the start of the seventeenth century, not long after the introduction of tulips into Britain, and it was used several times in John Parkinson's *Paradisi in Sole Paradisus Terrestris* of 1629. Florists' societies and their accompanying shows, also referred to as feasts (usually held in public houses and accompanied by much merriment), sprang up across the country, following an established trend in the Low Countries, and gathered momentum throughout the seventeenth and eighteenth centuries. The tulip was one of eight flowers to be categorized as florists' flowers, the others being carnations, pinks, auriculas, anemones, hyacinths, polyanthus and ranunculus (followed later by dahlias and pansies), and this select group was the subject of scrutiny on the showbench. I suppose that I am a florist in both the old and the new senses of the word. I arrange flowers – a little; I do not do it all day every day – and I am a specialist grower. I grow English Florists' tulips with the aim of keeping them in circulation and preventing them from becoming lost for future generations, and for exhibition.

Flower shows devoted entirely to the tulip came into existence in England in the middle of the eighteenth century (first documented in Suffolk), with the tulips largely imported from Holland and of the type included in our collection of Dutch Historic cultivars. By the early nineteenth century as many as two hundred tulip shows a year were being held across the country, and it was during this period that the English Florists' tulip came into being. New tulips were raised by seed from the cross-pollination of different cultivars and were subjected to rigorous and continuous selection in order to retain their most desirable characteristics: a shallow cup shape, petals of an even height, symmetrical markings and a clear base. The quest for the perfect tulip through hybridization was ongoing, the standards high and the competition intense.

The Wakefield and North of England Tulip Society (hereafter the Tulip Society) was established in 1836, but was probably operating even earlier, as local newspaper articles dating from 1829 document the staging of annual shows. At the end of the nineteenth century it was one of only four tulip societies still in existence after the English Florists' tulip took a dramatic downturn in popularity, partly owing to increasing industrialization and the loss of back gardens and allotments, and partly as a result of the new trend for the impressive Darwin types that had recently been introduced as bedding plants. Today the Tulip Society is the only such surviving society in the country. Its Annual Show, held in West Yorkshire each May, has become a place of pilgrimage for dedicated tulip-growers, myself included, who worship these most refined of flowers. The jewel-like colours and exquisite markings are improbably displayed in the most unrefined of vessels, a plain brown beer bottle (overleaf is a 'James Wainwright' breeder tulip, left, and a 'Habit de Noce' feather, right) – a hangover from the early days, when gatherings were held in pubs. The ritual of the beer bottle – its brown colour the best possible foil for the colours of the blooms – may hark back even further, to the time of Tulipmania in the seventeenth century, when deals would be brokered in the backstreets of Amsterdam or Haarlem for precious bulbs with blooms that had yet to be seen but were already believed. The Annual Show is followed a week or two later by the Small Show, to account for late or early seasons and give as many members as possible the chance to exhibit their tulips.

Membership of the Tulip Society consisted historically of working-class men (with an unexplained predominance of shoemakers), and the tulips were grown on allotments and small back garden plots. A non-commercial ethos was insisted on from the outset and continues today: bulbs can never be bought, but are instead distributed to members of the society once a year following the annual general meeting in October. As stated in *Flames and Feathers*, the definitive guide to English Florists' tulips, published by the society in 2012, 'success cannot be bought, ensuring a truly amateur society'.

I joined the society in 2016, went to my first show in 2018 and became brave enough to bring my tulips to be judged a year later. Today's members are a diverse group hailing from places as far-flung as Aberdeen and Bridport, and as (increasingly) remote from each other as Moscow and Maryland, with a strong contingent from Sweden. Anybody can pay the modest fee to become a member and receive the yearly newsletter, although the journey to the show in Wakefield is a deterrent to a high proportion of visitors. That said, there is the odd enthusiastic teenager who turns up with tulips to place on the showbench, and several unbelievably knowledgeable octogenarians who have been the lifeblood of the society for decades. Any initial concerns I had about being female, a southerner and middle-class were immediately expunged upon my first visit to the show, and a tulip tour of the Netherlands organized by the society a year later confirmed my opinion that there could not be a more inclusive group. The combined experience of the Officers of the Tulip Society amounts to many centuries of first-hand experience growing, showing and judging English Florists' tulips, and the expertise is freely and generously given – for, however appealing the competitive side of the society may be, the ulterior motive of all involved is to keep this highly superior breed of flowers alive in perpetuity.

As the renowned author, former president of the Tulip Society and hybridizer of tulips Daniel Hall wrote in *The Book of the Tulip* (1929), 'the longer one studies tulips the more does one incline to their [Florists' tulips] ordered and subtle beauty'. Their beauty is undeniable, I know of nothing else like them in the whole of the genus Tulipa, and this is because of the order that has been imposed on the tulips since their inception. English Florists' tulips come with a strict set of rules and standards that must be adhered to. These high standards have been continuously maintained because of the existence of the tulip shows at which the 'fanciers', as they were known, competed. There is nothing like a bit of stiff competition to keep exhibitors on their toes. No precise records point to a time when the rules and regulations were first enforced, but early periodicals tell of fierce disagreement between northern growers, who favoured the symmetry of markings and a clean base colour over everything else, and southerners, who focused primarily on the form of the flower. Londoners insisted that all aspects be given equal weight, and would accept no compromise. The formation of the National Tulip Society in 1849 helped to unite the different factions, and by the time of its demise in 1936 (when there were only two surviving members, despite the society having become 'Royal'), a strict set of criteria was fixed upon that remains much the same to this day. Upon its closure the Royal National Tulip Society handed over the baton and its coveted silverware to the Wakefield contingent, who continue to uphold standards.

The tulips are categorized into a limited palette of three colourways: Rose, Bybloemen and Bizarre (see opposite). A Rose tulip must have an underlying colour (known as the base or ground) of pure white, with pink to red colouring of the petals. 'Juliet' (c.1845) is a deep pink example that I grow, and 'Mabel', dating from about 1860, a paler, less intensely coloured one. A Bybloemen also has a clean white ground, but its overlying colour is always a shade of purple, from lilac through to deep purple, occasionally with a rosy hue. The relatively new 'Wendy Akers' is at the lighter end of the spectrum, and slaty blue 'Talisman' (c.1860) at the other. Bizarre tulips have a yellow ground with brown to red petals and are the most striking in appearance, although they were considered the least desirable colourway throughout much of the eighteenth century, most likely because of the prevalence of bright yellow tulips on the market.

Bizarres are my personal favourites. I find the combination of strong yellow and deep mahogany, as exemplified in 'James Wild' (c.1890) and 'Lord Stanley' (c.1860), bewitching. That said, a well-marked broken Bybloemen is also hard to beat. One that I grow, the late nineteenth-century 'Bessie', encapsulates my love for the precious English Florists' tulips, with dark purple flames licking over a white base. It has a dogged determination to flower beautifully each year, as well as generously giving me a clutch of healthy offsets to grow on.

Within each colourway of Rose, Bybloemen and Bizarre, the bulbs exist in both breeder and broken form, although sadly many English Florists' breeders have disappeared as a result of becoming infected by Tulip Breaking Virus (TBV), particularly those in the Rose category. Bizarres are a little better served in the breeder department, although I am experiencing frustrating breaking with 'James Wild', of which I have an ever-diminishing unbroken supply, despite my careful growing and handling practices. Breeders – also known as 'mother' bulbs (a term confusingly also used to describe a large bulb that produces offsets each

A trio of breeder tulips demonstrating the three
recognized colourways of English Florists' tulips:
Rose (top), Bizarre (centre) and Bybloemen (bottom).

The insides of a *Tulipa* 'James Wild' flame (left) and
T. 'Agbrigg' feather (right). The markings on the interior of a
broken tulip carry more weight than those on the exterior,
another reason the open hemispherical shape is favoured:
the judges must be able to have a good look inside.

year) – are typically of a lighter shade than the broken version, where the overlying layer of anthocyanin is significantly deeper in colour. This makes the markings of a broken tulip even more dramatic, but can lead to confusion when trying to identify a rogue bloom. The committee members of the Tulip Society are always happy to help, and it is a good idea to take any mystery English Florists' tulips to the Annual Show for their expert opinion. There are roughly equal numbers of breeder and broken bulbs within my collection, with a loose balance between the three colourways and a slant towards later-flowering cultivars, such as the striking Bizarre 'Sir Joseph Paxton' (c.1850, see p.167).

Once you have got your head around the fact that there are three different colourways, and that each can be represented by a breeder or broken flower, it is time to address the markings. Broken English Florists' tulips should, ideally, be flamed or feathered (see opposite). I say ideally because that is the aim and that is how the classes in the Annual Show schedule are structured. In reality, however, perfect markings are few and far between, and for every tulip that has desirable markings there will be many that fall short. One class at the show, for the prestigious Needham Memorial Cup, asks for a stand of twelve rectified (broken) English tulips, all dissimilar, consisting of four Bizarres (two flamed and two feathered), four Bybloemens (two flamed and two feathered) and four Roses (yes, two flamed and two feathered); preference is given to twelve different varieties of the same quality. To produce an entry for this class takes a lifetime of experience. I have managed to produce entries for the single-bloom classes, 'One Flamed' or 'One Feathered', a few times, and in 2023 I finally entered the class 'Pan of Three, one Breeder, one Flamed, one Feathered'.

In a feathered flower the markings are restricted to the edges of the petal, and should be in a finely drawn, unbroken line. In the words of Daniel Hall, 'in a feathered flower the marking ... should be continuous and finely pencilled, but its depth may vary considerably with the variety.' This is often accompanied by a stripe down the central beam of the petal, called a thumbmark, but the aim is for the overlying colour (the one that forms the markings) to be limited to the far reaches of the petal. Gaps in the feathering at the edges of the petal are called 'skips', and are undesirable.

A flamed flower has the central beam as the starting point, from which markings will branch and connect with the feathering at the edges of the petal. In both flames and feathers symmetry is essential, so that the markings are spread evenly across the flower both inside and out, with a light touch. The underlying colour (yellow in a Bizarre) should shine through uniformly, without being obscured by solid patches of the darker breeder colour. Any rectified tulip showing 'black break', a solid, high concentration of overlying colour, is to be destroyed.

Good flames are more common (if that is a word that can ever be applied to English Florists' tulips) than good feathers, and more likely to come true year on year. I have yet to bring a feather that I am proud of to the show, partly because my southern-grown tulips tend to bloom too early, although I have had some fine feathers that have given me – their admiring audience of one – immense satisfaction. A noteworthy feather will draw a tight huddle of judges at the show and a murmur of anticipation from the competitors, who, until the judging is finished, are confined to the periphery of the room, enjoying the spread that is the present-day equivalent of the Florists' Feast of centuries earlier.

The strict rules imposed by the Tulip Society appeal to my perfectionist nature. I pore over my English Florists' collection in the run-up to the Annual Show each May, trying to decide which individual flowers are likely to perform best. Burrowing beneath the netting that protects the plants from the weather, I examine the breeder and broken beds at increasingly frequent intervals, trying to ascertain where the strengths lie. Each year is different. Sometimes I will have a strong showing of Rose breeders, among them 'Judy Baker' and 'Utopia' (both early twenty-first century), but a year later broken Bybloemens, such as 'Adonis' (c.1850) and 'Agbrigg' (c.1970), will come to the fore. In an ideal situation I would be able to produce a good representation from across the collection, all at their peak, to enter a wide range of classes – but for now that remains a fantasy rather than reality.

The Annual Show schedule currently contains thirty-six different classes. Apart from a few Dutch Vase classes at the start (which I also enter enthusiastically), the competition is purely for English Florists' tulips. Fifteen 'Open' classes create complex challenges for the expert grower, who must produce 'pans', 'stands' and 'stages' of different combinations of tulips. 'Seedling' classes are for hybrids that have been recently bred from seed (as opposed to being propagated by offset), as yet unnamed and posing exciting possibilities of a future cultivar to join the much-admired ranks. In addition are the 'Novice' and 'Extra Open' classes, which the less experienced members can enter, and it is these at which I try my hand, for although I have an ever-growing collection and all the enthusiasm that can be mustered, I am still very much a newcomer at this game. To become a respected prize-winner takes time, patience and a willingness to learn and make mistakes – as I found out when an entry I made was marked down for containing a rogue tulip of a different variety, identifiable by the presence of blue in its base. I felt utterly humiliated by the experience, but was greatly cheered when reading through the archives of the Tulip Society to discover that the same experience had befallen other exhibitors, including a past editor of the annual newsletter.

Regardless of which class an English Florists' tulip falls into, its quality must be the very highest. In 1929 Hall wrote, 'The ideal shape is defined as the half of a hollow ball, but a true hemisphere is somewhat shallower in the cup than is usual or desirable, and the typical shape lies somewhere between the hemisphere and the shape of a claret glass', an opinion that is still held today. The markings on the inside of a tulip are considered as important, if not more so, than those on the outside, and the shallower the flower, the more visible the interior will be. 'James Wainwright' (a recent introduction) is more claret-glass-shaped than most (indeed, it is also the colour of claret, and has the appearance of a full glass of wine), while 'Casius', another relative newcomer raised by the same breeder, John Wainwright, is satisfyingly hemispherical. Gone are the days when crinolines of wood shavings would be used to maintain the open shape of the tulip before it was placed on the showbench, although competitors can still be seen gently breathing warm air on to a stubbornly closed specimen or – as I did in 2023 – placing it in shafts of sunlight on a windowsill, to encourage it to open in time for the judging.

Petals should be rounded at the top; they might be notched – see 'James Wild' – but should never be pointed. The stubbier they are, the better. They should be equal in height, without gaps at the base (known as 'quartering'), as well as velvety smooth and of good density. A paper-thin petal is not acceptable, however whimsically beautiful it might appear to the casual observer. An English Florists' tulip must always have six petals and six stamens, a point I have (once) overlooked in the run-up to the show and been marked down on. The stamens of every flower really are counted as they are judged, and woe betide the entrant who accidentally knocks one off while using a dampened paintbrush to clean pollen from the base of the tulip.

The base is one of the most prized parts of the tulip, acting as a mount for the markings of a broken example or the main colour of a breeder. It can be round or star-shaped, depending on the cultivar, as long as it is pure white (in a Rose or Bybloemen) or yellow (in a Bizarre), and never blue. I made the mistake of buying some 'Columbine' bulbs from a wholesale source a few years ago, and the blue halo around the base gave away the fact that they were not the accepted strain for the Tulip Society. Whether or not off-white was allowed was a hotly contested point between northern and southern tulip-fanciers in the nineteenth century, finally settled in favour of the all-white southern brigade.

The Annual Show is held on the first or second weekend of May, nearly always on a Saturday. By this time of year the species tulips and most of the garden hybrids have finished flowering, leaving the Single Late division (Division 5), into which English Florists' tulips fall – indeed, they are the latest of the lates. I find this timing a challenge, since the climate in the south of England is milder than in the north, where the show is held and where the majority of growers live. My solution is to plant the tulips late in December, rather than in November, in order to delay flowering. James Akers, one of the most experienced growers and showers of the Tulip Society and one of its Patrons, gave me this advice, along with a raft of other helpful information, when I first joined. The late planting helps, but a prolonged period of spring warmth can still bring them on too quickly, so it is often necessary to cut them at their peak and refrigerate them for a few days before the show.

I occasionally wonder whether all the angst associated with growing and showing English Florists' tulips is worth it, but the jolt of sheer delight they give me every year when they come into flower and I see them afresh reassures me that it is a pleasure worth pursuing. No other flower that I know or grow exhibits such purity of form, depth of colour and refinement of markings. Rather like my children, they deserve all the attention they demand of me.

Opposite: *Tulipa* 'Mabel' in a Dutch Delft *tulipière* dating
from about 1700. This English Florists' tulip cultivar is a
regular prize-winner at the Annual Show.

Breeder and Broken Tulips

T. 'ADONIS'

T. 'AGBRIGG'

T. 'ALBERT TEAR'

T. 'BESSIE'

T. 'CASIUS'

T. 'COLUMBINE'

T. 'JACK TAYLOR'

T. 'JAMES WILD'

T. 'JUDY BAKER'

T. 'JULIA FARNESE'

T. 'JULIET'

T. 'LORD STANLEY'

T. 'MABEL'

T. 'MUSIC'

T. 'SIR JOSEPH PAXTON'

T. 'SOLIS'

T. 'TALISMAN'

T. 'WENDY AKERS'

ENGLISH FLORISTS' TULIPS, as with Dutch Historics (see Chapter 2), are divided into two groups: breeders, which are solid-coloured and unaffected by TBV, and broken (or rectified), which have been infected by TBV and have distinct markings where the overlying colour (anthocyanin) has broken to reveal the underlying base colour. The markings of broken tulips are subdivided into flamed or feathered categories. In a feathered flower the markings are confined to the outside edges of the petal, and should appear as a continuous feathered line; a flamed one has a central beam of contrasting colour up the centre of the petal, from which the markings radiate to the feathered perimeters.

Each cultivar corresponds to one of three colourways: Rose, Bybloemen or Bizarre (see p.150). A Rose tulip has a pure white base and pink to red petals, Bybloemens have a white base with petals in shades of purple and Bizarres have yellow bases with red to brown petals, verging on black in some cases. The bases, whether white or yellow, must be unadulterated by another colour, and the markings

on the petals of a broken tulips should be clean, with no bleeding of one colour to another. Purity of form and markings is key to these rarefied tulips. These colourways play a part in the classes at the Tulip Society's Annual Show, and are therefore crucial for English Florists' tulips in a way that they are not for Dutch Historics.

Highlights from my collection are organized alphabetically in this section, and are represented by a breeder, flamed or feathered example – or something in between, since I am still striving for perfection. Each profile indicates whether a breeder or broken example is illustrated – 'James Wild' is pictured opposite in all three 'stages': breeder, flame and feather. Breeders are classified as Single Late (Division 5), and flamed or feathered as Rembrandt (Division 9). They are all late to flower; some are later than others, and these have been noted. Here (unlike in previous chapters), I do not give heights. Height is not actually relevant, since these tulips are grown for the showbench, and always presented with the flower head resting directly on the top of the beer bottle.

T. 'ADONIS'
Bybloemen (broken)

Deep purple-black markings on a pure white ground, with a tendency to produce better feathers than flames (see opposite, top left). The petals are a little papery, which can result in a less defined form as they age, and shrivelled tips in warmer weather. That said, this is an exquisite tulip with beautiful colouring, a long, slender stem and attractive, narrow leaves. 'Adonis' was offered for sale in *Barr's General Bulb Catalogue* of 1906 as both broken and breeder, 'finely feathered and lightly flamed purple and black on a dazzling white ground', but I have only ever seen it in broken form and think it unlikely that the breeder still exists. The man who raised it, Richard Headly of Stapleford House near Cambridge, cultivated auriculas, carnations and picotees in addition to tulips.

DATE: Raised by Richard Headly, *c*.1850
FLOWERING TIME: April

T. 'AGBRIGG'
Bybloemen (broken)

Purple to the point of black (and referred to as black in *Flames and Feathers*) on a white ground, with a propensity to produce good feathers (see opposite, below left). It was awarded Premier Bloom at the Annual Show in 2023 for a feather, and flames are improving in quality. The petals are slightly more elongated than the ideal hemispherical shape, veering towards claret-glass, but this is deemed acceptable. Named after a suburb of Wakefield by the man who bred it, Hubert Calvert, a member of the Tulip Society for nearly fifty years and its secretary. Calvert described his growing conditions thus: 'My plot is on the North side of our semi-detached council house, with a slight slope away from the house. The soil is a mixture of what the builders dumped on it and contains a lot of flat stones of various sizes. Because of this it is impossible to dig with a spade and I always use a garden fork.' 'Agbrigg' is no longer available as a breeder.

DATE: Raised by Hubert Calvert, *c*.1970; named in 1976
FLOWERING TIME: Late April–May

T. 'ALBERT TEAR'
Bybloemen (breeder)

This deep magenta breeder (also available as a break) is a relative newcomer, hailing from 1960, when, according to *Flames and Feathers*, it was discovered as a sport growing among Albert Tear's Bybloemen breeders, seemingly having hybridized from existing stock (see opposite, top right). I enjoy the story of its lifting: 'When being dug up the spade went through the bulb and left it in four parts. It has survived and is reasonably widely distributed among the members.' It grows well for me (also increasing well, producing decent-sized offsets), although I find the shape of its head slightly square compared to most other English Florists' tulips. The base is small and starry, bright white and clearly visible on the outside, the stem long. I take all the correct precautions to keep this tulip unbroken, but secretly hope that it might one day produce a good flame, which it is apparently capable of doing.

DATE: Raised by Albert Tear in 1960
FLOWERING TIME: Late April–early May

T. 'BESSIE'
Bybloemen (breeder)

'Bessie' is available in breeder and broken forms, and we have both in our collection. The breeder is a brilliant plummy purple with a rosy tint (indeed, it is known as a Rosy Bybloemen, see opposite, below right), the broken version even deeper purple with a predominance of heavily marked flames over feathers. It is one of the most striking Bybloemens, and possibly my favourite, thanks to its rich markings. Despite its relatively short stature – *Barr's General Bulb Catalogue* of 1908 describes it as 'dwarf' – this is a robust tulip that multiplies well with plentiful offsets of a good size. The petals have a tendency to reflex as the flower ages, a trait that is acknowledged in the description given by the Tulip Society in *Flames and Feathers*, and reassures me that mine are not substandard (although the markings might be considered as such). The base starts off yellowish-white, maturing to a clean white over the flowering period. 'Bessie' has been awarded the sought-after Premier Bloom cup in the Annual Show for a flamed flower. John Hepworth, who bred it, was a nineteenth-century florist from Yorkshire who raised both auriculas and tulips.

DATE: Raised by John Hepworth in the late nineteenth century
FLOWERING TIME: Late April–May

T. 'CASIUS'
Rose (breeder)

Deep rose-red, with a classic half-cup-shaped flower head of generous proportions (see opposite, top left). The base is large and brightest white, coming to a small point in the centre of each petal; the stigma is large and the anthers substantial, with thick purple-black pollen (which scatters on the base and takes time to remove with a dampened paintbrush for the showbench). The mid-green leaves are slightly undulate. It is tall for an English Florists' tulip, and I find it a very healthy cultivar that performs well and offers decent offsets alongside a good mother bulb each year; its only weakness is to mark badly from hailstones, a problem that can be mitigated by erecting proper covers in good time. 'Casius' often features in prize-winning stands of breeders at the Annual Show, and produces some good flowers in its broken form, too. Breeders in the Rose colourway were in short supply until John Wainwright bred a much-needed range of new ones in the 1990s, and this is one of my favourites.

DATE: Raised by John Wainwright in the early twenty-first century
FLOWERING TIME: May

T. 'COLUMBINE'
Bybloemen (breeder)

In its breeder form 'Columbine' is a quiet flower that does not clamour for attention, pale heliotrope in colour (see opposite, below left), but as a break it is spectacular, with markings of deep magenta-purple against bright white. Capable of producing excellent flames and feathers, it is a strong contender for the Stages Cup at the Annual Show. I grow both breeder and broken versions, and admit to having a penchant for a feather, where the contrasting colourways can be seen in all their glory – but this tulip is early to flower, so I have not yet managed to take it to the show. The influential botanical artist Rory McEwen (1932–1983) painted both a breeder and a feathered flower in Wilfred Blunt's *Tulips and Tulipomania* in 1977, so he was evidently keen on it, too. A version of 'Columbine' is sometimes available from commercial sources, but it tends to have highly irregular markings and a blue tinge to the base, and is not recognized by the Tulip Society.

DATE: Raised by Sir Daniel Hall, c.1920
FLOWERING TIME: April–May

T. 'JACK TAYLOR'
Bizarre (breeder)

Mahogany-brown petals, a little darker at the margins and with a prominent midrib (see opposite, top right). The interior of the inner three is slightly notched and has a yellowish stripe at the centre. A large, bright yellow base has at its middle an oversized, coral-like stigma. The wide leaves are not the most attractive, but must help to provide energy for the sizeable new bulbs that are produced each year. Tall and vigorous (in common with many of the newer hybrids), 'Jack Taylor' was named after the esteemed exhibitor and judge who died shortly after the Annual Show in 2009, at which this tulip had been awarded Premier Breeder while exhibited under the seedling number E92-20. It makes a useful entry in its breeder form, and has recently seen success in its broken form as a flame.

DATE: Raised by John Wainwright in 2009
FLOWERING TIME: May

T. 'JAMES WILD'
Bizarre (broken)

Most probably named after James Wilde, a grower who exhibited his tulips at flower shows in Lancashire in the nineteenth century, this tulip is present in our collection in both breeder and broken forms, producing striking flamed and feathered flowers (see opposite, below right). Unbroken, the petals are deep chestnut-brown, the base a clear yellow, with the faintest of yellow streaks scoring delicate lines up the centres of the petals and around the rims. The inner petals are notched, making them appear heart-shaped rather than round, a detail that helps to distinguish this cultivar from the almost identical 'Sulphur'. Strong stems, more robust than those of many English Florists' tulips, make it a good choice for a container planting. 'James Wild' breaks too readily and generally quite heavily, with large patches of solid colour (a type of break known as 'black break'). It is therefore of particular importance to plant the breeder bulbs at a considerable distance from the broken ones. A feathered 'James Wild' was awarded Premier Bloom at the Annual Show in 2018, and this tulip regularly wins Best Flame and Feather.

DATE: Raised by James Walker, c.1890
FLOWERING TIME: Late April–May

T. 'JUDY BAKER'
Rose (breeder)

Rich rose with a substantial white base and elegant, evenly spaced anthers (see opposite, top left). While the petals are of nicely rounded form (although marginally longer than those of 'Solis'), the ones I grow can be slightly notched and uneven. John Wainwright sent bulbs of this tulip as a seedling (an unnamed new hybrid) to Judy Baker, a successful exhibitor and vice-president of the Tulip Society, to help her achieve the required number of entries for the 12 Breeders class, and later named it after her. I do not have any breaks to date, although I will request some at the next annual bulb exchange. In 2011 it won Premier Feather at the Annual Show, and it makes regular appearances in all three forms as breeder, flame and feather.

DATE: Raised by John Wainwright in the early twenty-first century
FLOWERING TIME: Late April–early May

T. 'JULIA FARNESE'
Rose (broken)

'Julia Farnese', with cherry-red markings on a bright white ground, is exhibited at the Annual Show as both a flame and a feather, but is no longer found as a breeder (see opposite, below left). As a flamed flower it often presents without the central beam up the centre of the petal; as a feather it is frequently 'plated', meaning that there is a thick, solid body of colour towards the outside of the petal, as opposed to a finer, more delicate line. A 'Julia Farnese' feather was beautifully painted by Rory McEwen for the revised edition of Wilfred Blunt's book *Tulips & Tulipomania* (1977). McEwen was a highly respected patron of the Tulip Society, as well as being a well-known folk singer and sculptor. There is an English Florists' tulip, raised by James Akers, named 'Rory McEwen' in his memory. A 'Julia Farnese' was awarded Best Feather at the Annual Show in 2012 and again in 2022, as well as the Cochrane of Cults Vase for Best Bloom in classes 23–25. John Slater, who raised this cultivar, was the author of *A Descriptive Catalogue of Tulips* (1843), a very useful reference work in my library.

DATE: Raised by John Slater, *c*.1853
FLOWERING TIME: Late April–May

T. 'JULIET'
Synonym: *T.* 'Juliette'
Rose (breeder)

The earliest English Florists' tulip that I grow, and one of the prettiest with a perfect head shape (see opposite, top right), this tulip is best appreciated when fully open. A clear, vibrant rose colour with a cream base, brightening to white as the flower ages. It produces a poor flamed flower, but it regularly wins classes as a breeder at the Annual Show, including Premier Bloom in 2019. William Willison, the raiser, was a prominent nurseryman of Whitby who exhibited regularly at shows and contributed articles to the key periodicals of the day. In the 1852 issue of *The Midland Florist*, he writes of 'the firm and majestic strides the tulip fancy is taking through the length and breadth of our island. I may mention one circumstance as a striking proof of this – that parties (first-rate growers) ordering my seedling rose breeder, Juliet, have preferred to pay in cash, rather than with good varieties from their collections, which they might have done.' Exchanging varieties is once again the mode of transaction.

DATE: Raised by William Willison, *c*.1845
FLOWERING TIME: Late April–early May

T. 'LORD STANLEY'
Bizarre (broken)

Regal red with a strong yellow base, this tulip is a regular award-winner at the Annual Show, having won Best Flame three times since 2018 (see opposite, below right). Described in *Flames and Feathers* as 'the most prolific and consistent flower grown today which, although often first out on the bed, is the last to die', it also has the unusual merit of not burning in sunshine. The shape of the breeder is not perfect, but what it lacks in form it makes up for with outstanding flames and the occasional noteworthy feather. *Barr's General Bulb Catalogue* had no issue with the shape, describing the breeder as a 'flower of fine form with short broad petals', and the broken version as 'very prettily flamed and feathered mahogany-crimson on a bright yellow ground'. The top part of the stem is stained burgundy, as if the colour has bled out of the flower head. Tom Storer, who raised this prized cultivar, was a successful tulip exhibitor from Derby who is thought to have worked as a railway engine fitter.

DATE: Raised by Tom Storer, *c*.1860
FLOWERING TIME: Mid-April–early May

T. 'MABEL'
Rose (broken)

'Mabel' is a stalwart of the Annual Show, having won Premier Bloom as breeder and feather (see opposite, top left). It also produces a good flame. The cup is slightly elongated, but that has not hindered the success of this cultivar, nor has the fact that the petals incurve marginally (known as 'hooking', as can be seen in this photograph of the broken version). They do this in regular fashion and are equally sized, so the overall effect is symmetrical and pleasing. The breeder is rose-pink in hue, darkening considerably in the broken form to a deep cherry-red on a white ground. The leaves are gently undulating or wavy-edged. A few years ago, I made the mistake of purchasing some bulbs of 'Mabel' from a commercial source; they were very badly marked and almost unrecognizable as an English Florists' tulip. These inferior examples are now grown in a separate bed and I cut them freely to use in my personal floristry work, where they are always greatly admired. The bulbs I received from the Tulip Society are entirely different beasts, and sacrosanct, and they are only ever cut for exhibiting on the showbench.

DATE: Raised by John Martin, c.1864
FLOWERING TIME: Late April–early May

T. 'MUSIC'
Bybloemen (breeder)

A substantial flower, in both height and head size, with a somewhat square base (see opposite, below left). The petals are slightly elongated, less rounded than those of most English Florists' tulips, but the flower wears them well. Vibrant magenta purple in colour against a white ground. The supersized twisted stigma, which resembles a stick of brain coral, helps to differentiate it from other Bybloemens, which can look remarkably similar to one another. Anthers are jet-black, long and unruly-looking, and the basal leaves are unusually wide. I have been growing 'Music' for a number of years and it has not produced any breaks, which is no great pity since it has a tendency to produce markings of poor quality.

DATE: Raised by David Jackson, c.1860
FLOWERING TIME: Late April–May

T. 'SIR JOSEPH PAXTON'
Bizarre (broken)

Burgundy-brown on a lemon-yellow ground, a little paler than most other Bizarres and its head somewhat larger (see opposite, top right). 'Sir Joseph Paxton' is represented in our collection as a flame, although to date I have not had a specimen with perfect markings (and the petals of mine tend to recurve as they age). The breeder is no longer in existence, despite attempts to restore it through selection. It has a strong track record at the Annual Show, repeatedly being awarded Best Flame, most recently in 2022 with an entry by Chris Gill. In *The English Florists' Tulip*, published by the Tulip Society in 1997, we are told that 'For 150 years it ['Sir Joseph Paxton'] has been one of the best flames and a regular premier bloom in show. Also produces on occasions a good feather.' It flowers later than most tulips in my collection, and is therefore a good bet for me to exhibit. Joseph Paxton was an architect and gardener who rose from humble beginnings to become head gardener at Chatsworth House in Derbyshire. He designed the great conservatory there in the late 1830s and subsequently the Crystal Palace for the Great Exhibition of 1851 – for which he received a knighthood from Queen Victoria.

DATE: Raised by William Willison, c.1850
FLOWERING TIME: May

T. 'SOLIS'
Rose (breeder)

Bright rose-pink with a hint of lilac, this hue most pronounced on the insides of the petals (see opposite, below right). The flower head is on the small side, slightly elongated, and the petals recurve a little as they mature. While the base is pure white (as it should be with the Rose colouration), it is not sharply defined and morphs gently into the petal colour. The tiny stigma is at the centre of a ring of long, narrow, pale purple anthers. Leaves are light green and the stem quite short – although this (and the small flower head) could be because I have been growing 'Solis' only since 2022; it may still bulk up and grow taller. In its broken form, lightly marked flames of cream flicker up the centres of the petals. I grow both versions, but the broken ones have yet to produce any blooms with markings worthy of the showbench – although other exhibitors fare well with it.

DATE: Raised by John Wainwright in the early twenty-first century
FLOWERING TIME: May

T. 'TALISMAN'
Bybloemen (breeder and broken)

'Talisman' sits in our collection at Blacklands in both its breeder and broken forms. The breeder is a dull plum colour on a pure white ground, which darkens to almost black against shards of white as a flamed break; the few feathers that bloom for me are poorly marked and not of sufficient quality to show. It is a most striking tulip of impressive stature, late to flower yet long-lasting, the stems slender yet strong. It copes well with bad weather, although I still cover it with netting to preserve its petals for the showbench. The cup is pleasingly hemispherical, but as the tulip matures the three inner petals grow slightly longer and the outer ones start to reflex (as can be seen in the photograph of the break), thus spoiling the symmetry. In 1929 Daniel Hall remarked, 'For more than fifty years "Talisman" has been pre-eminent in its class, both as a feathered and a flamed flower.' It continues to pick up prizes today, being awarded Premier Bloom at the Annual Show in 2021. Dr D. W. Hardy, who raised 'Talisman' (and very soon afterwards, in 1862, had a *T.* 'Doctor Hardy' named after him by Tom Storer), distinguished himself in the field of midwifery. He was instrumental in stipulating the standards by which an English Florists' tulip should be judged, along with George Glenny, author of *The Culture of Flowers and Plants* (1860).

DATE: Raised by Dr D. W. Hardy, *c.*1860
FLOWERING TIME: May

T. 'WENDY AKERS'
Bybloemen (breeder)

A very light-coloured Bybloemen in a luminescent lilac-pink, overlaid by a slightly deeper shade at the centre of each petal that finishes in a point at the tip; this creates a subtle margin of the palest lilac. The three inner petals have a faint double line of white at the midrib, on the exterior surface only. The base is even in shape yet undefined, owing to the light colouration, and white fades into the overlying petal colour. Jet-black anthers stand in stark contrast. This is another of the recent introductions made by John Wainwright, and I find it a very reliable tulip that produces good flowers year after year, and does not break readily. It was named after the late Wendy Akers, a highly respected vice-president of the Tulip Society. In 2023 this cultivar was included in the prize-winning stands for the Eyre Family Trophy and the Royles Jubilee Cup at the Annual Show (both classes for breeders, both won by Judy Baker).

DATE: Raised by John Wainwright in the early twenty-first century
FLOWERING TIME: May

Growing English Florists' Tulips

In almost every respect our English Florists' tulips are grown in the same way as the Dutch Historics (see p.137), but they do need more shelter from the weather to keep them pristine. As they come into bud we erect over-the-beds structures formed of hazel rods covered with a fine mesh, to protect the flowers from hail, wind and sunshine. Hailstorms can destroy a flower by leaving unsightly pockmarks all over the petals, and have a nasty habit of descending on us just before the show each year. Wind is all well and good during the first stages of a tulip's growth – in fact it helps to increase airflow in the beds and strengthens the stems – but once a flower is in full bloom it can cause irreparable damage. Sunshine is the factor that surprised me when I started growing show tulips in earnest. I assumed it would be beneficial, but it turns out that not only does it leach the colours, lessening the vibrancy and contrast of the markings, but also it ages the petals prematurely by repeatedly encouraging them to open wide and close again. Tulips must be planted in full sun, but need shielding from it once they are in flower.

As with the Dutch Historics, it is vital that the beds of broken tulips are at a considerable distance from those for breeders. It is no understatement to say that this is the most important factor in growing English Florists' tulips, and be sure to handle the breeder bulbs before the broken ones during the whole process of lifting, sorting and storing.

On the eve of the show I cut the best of the blooms, making sure the leaves stay on the plant to photosynthesize and create energy for the new mother bulb that will form before lifting in July. The leaves are not necessary for showing the tulips, since the flower head sits straight on the neck of the beer bottle on the showbench. For the same reason, the stem can be quite short, although I like it to be a few inches long so that I can transport the tulips in water to keep them as fresh as possible. It is a long journey, and I find that they keep best if they are hydrated, in the dark recesses of a giant cool box stowed in the boot of the car.

Once the show is over and I am back home, the tulips left in the beds are released from their protective covers and I carry out a quality-control audit, assessing which flowers look less than healthy, and which have produced substandard markings (having photographed and noted the ones that were cut for the show). Those that fall below the high standards maintained by the Tulip Society are destroyed, while particularly fine examples are marked so that their offsets can be given extra-special care. Good markings on a tulip will be passed on to the next generation when propagating by offset, particularly in the case of a flamed flower – feathers are less reliable – and it is through this process of selection that the quality of tulips can be controlled.

As with the Dutch Historics, any breeder that breaks (and produces good markings) is marked with a coloured thread and moved to the broken stock when the bulbs are lifted. Propagating by seed is a slow process, and the seed does not come true, so I prefer to deadhead all the flowers and increase stocks by offsets, even if that means a very gradual increase by one or two bulbs each year. I am, however, starting to experiment with the hybridization of English Florists' tulips, with the hope of raising new seedlings. The fruits of this process will not be evident for up to seven years, which is the time it can take for a tulip to flower from seed. That does not deter me. I am in this for the long game.

IV

Annual Tulips

Detail of a large-scale arrangement featuring annual tulips, including
'Dream Touch', 'Charming Lady', 'Black Hero', 'La Belle Époque' and
'Continental'. Pages 176–7: Annual tulips in flower in the walled garden,
including 'Stunning Apricot', 'Black Hero' and 'Maureen'.

Annual tulips, otherwise known as garden or hybrid tulips, are far and away the most commonly seen tulips in gardens and parks. They are the tulip that springs to mind whenever the word is mentioned, conjuring an image of a simple flower, usually red, with three petals, two symmetrical leaves and a tall, straight stem. Planted conventionally as mass bedding in blocks of colour, or intermingled with other spring plants in mixed borders, they signify the height of spring and the lengthening of the days.

The British nation's love affair with annual tulips began after the Dutch nursery owner E. H. Krelage launched a new range of Flemish tulips named Darwins (after the naturalist Charles Darwin) at the Exposition Universelle in Paris in 1889. Planted en masse, as bedding, in rivers of breathtaking colour around the Trocadero Palace, they captured the public's imagination. Since then countless new cultivars have been bred by hybridization and selective breeding, and the annual tulip has become popular to the point of being fetishized. The climax each year is the tulip festival held at Keukenhof in the Netherlands, to which tulip-lovers from the world over flock to admire in excess of 7 million bulbs in full bloom.

The United Kingdom imports millions of tulip bulbs from Holland every year (318 million in 2022), as well as producing a limited number of home-grown bulbs. Gardeners have been lured into the habit of replacing almost all these bulbs annually with fresh stock, and do so without questioning the validity of such an approach, or indeed its environmental impact. Commercial tulip bulbs are the foie-gras geese of the flower world. They are sold at the point where they are fit to burst, having been force-fed with chemicals over successive seasons to produce the juiciest bulbs possible, to explode in a dazzling display of colour and form.

The catch, however, is that so much artificial energy has gone in to creating this unnatural bulb for a one-off display that it is spent after flowering, and the bulb formed in readiness for the following year – for tulip bulbs replace themselves year on year – is much diminished in size and produces a correspondingly smaller flower. It cannot sustain itself. The expectation is that we will constantly replenish our borders and beds with newly bought bulbs, enjoy a spectacle of perfect uniformity, then dig them all up and throw them away. The work required to sustain such a practice is considerable, the cost significant and the waste lamentable, meaning that it's profitable for the bulb industry, but not so good for the gardener or the environment.

It is possible – and preferable – to adopt a different approach, to grow annual tulips in a more perennial, sustainable way. I have shunned the traditional use of hybrid tulips as bedding at Blacklands, focusing instead on establishing species tulips, such as *Tulipa sylvestris* and *T.* 'Peppermintstick' (both in the Miscellaneous division, Division 15), in many of our herbaceous and mixed borders (see Chapter 1). Hybrids do still play a role throughout the garden, and they are used in three different ways: first, in a vast array of containers; second, as perennial plantings, in the driveway for example, that flower over several seasons; and finally, in productive beds in the flower field and the walled garden to supply my business, Bayntun Flowers, with cut blooms.

There is a cyclical nature to the way we grow tulips that does not eliminate the joy of ordering new bulbs, but does mean that we keep our expenditure and consumption in check by recycling a percentage of them. New tulips are ordered each year for the containers, and when they have finished flowering my favourites are lifted, dried in racks over the summer, then replanted in late autumn in various sites throughout the garden for perennial displays. Tulips that I rate, but which do not fit into the more permanent garden schemes, are dried, cleaned and packed into hessian bags as presents for friends and family, or donated to charitable causes. Finally, those few that do nothing for me are thrown on to the compost heap to play their part in feeding the soil. Bulbs that have been cultivated for cut flowers cannot be recycled at all, since the blooms are picked from the base of the stem with their leaves attached and the plant is therefore unable to absorb the nutrients necessary for the creation of next season's bulb. In fact, we tend to harvest tulips for cut flowers with the bulb still attached, as that provides a few additional inches of stem.

This method of rehoming bulbs as perennials within the garden results in displays with a more naturalistic feel, since the flowers are diminished in size for their first year at least. I now prefer the effect created by the randomized heights and head sizes, to the extent that I would find it hard to live with a uniform new planting in the garden, in much the same way that I would find it hard to arrange a bunch of imported flowers. Every so often we supplement our perennial plantings with new bulbs, but this is kept to a minimum. The naturalistic effect that is created works with the garden as a whole entity, a space that is highly considered but soft at the edges, even slightly 'undone'. Some of the repurposed hybrid varieties bulk up by their second or third year to repeat-flower reliably, while others dwindle to nothing as the bulb divides into several bulblets that produce one or two leaves but no flowers. It gradually becomes evident which cultivars are suited to life in the wild and which prefer to be kept captive in containers, and we have built up a substantial list of what we refer to as perennial tulips (see p.241). This will vary from garden to garden, being dependent on soil type, aspect and climate, but if you persevere you will find a range of garden hybrids to greet you as familiar friends every year.

Cultivated tulips provide me with an endless palette of colour and form to play with throughout the garden, in an environmentally friendly fashion. The various traits – in terms of both behaviour and appearance – offered by the sixteen divisions into which they are classified (see p.223) mean that there are countless options. At Blacklands, tulips grown in containers are, for the most part, recycled for naturalized perennial plantings, while those grown as cut flowers offer a low-carbon option to local customers, with their stripped leaves and spent bulbs augmenting our compost heap.

Annual tulips for containers

Choosing annual tulips for containers offers unlimited freedom for self-expression and experimentation, although with between 6,000 and 7,000 hybrid tulips currently in cultivation, of which about 2,500 are commercially available, the process can be overwhelming. Bulb catalogues start dropping through the letter box in high summer, and the pressure rises from then on. If you procrastinate, the tulip you really, really wanted

may be sold out, so – as with most things in life – it is better to get on with it and place your orders early; you can always top up in the autumn, when a blitz of emails offer all bulbs at 30 per cent off, and your missing tulip has suddenly reappeared. I recommend that you don't buy what is currently most in fashion, since it is quite likely to be replaced with an alternative, less desirable tulip as the bulb companies run out of stock (a reputable supplier would never do this deliberately, but others do). Better to choose an often-overlooked old variety that won't be found on Instagram and will be in good supply. 'Apricot Beauty', a soft salmon-coloured Single Early (Division 1) tulip registered in 1953, is one example that is readily obtained, long-flowering and tolerant of shade, but not too obviously in vogue. Create fashions rather than following them and you will end up with far more interesting displays.

Before pressing the checkout button, it is important to assess the containers that you have, and where they will be positioned in the garden. I have accumulated a vast array of vessels over the years, from petite flowerpots that will house a single leftover bulb to enormous planters that hold more than 250 tulips and stand sentinel at the main points of entry to the garden. They range from salt-glaze pottery bowls to battered copper cauldrons, and from vintage metal dolly tubs to carved stone sinks, but the majority are made of terracotta, which has proved to be the most practical, affordable and readily available material. Terracotta is made from high-density clay and is both frost-resistant and porous, allowing the soil to retain moisture during a dry spell without becoming waterlogged in periods of excessive rain. The one thing that all our containers have in common is that they are made of strong, natural materials and are expected to last for many years.

Once we have chosen which containers to use, we start to create combinations of tulips, focusing on an entirely different palette each year while making sure that the tulips will all flower at approximately the same time. The garden is full of species tulips in March and early April, and these delicate, diminutive varieties deserve to be focused on without the distraction of great, strapping garden cultivars towering over them. The last two weeks of April have therefore become peak hybrid tulip period at Blacklands, when the containers and perennial displays flower in a riot of colour and form beneath the myriad apple and pear blossoms, and we open the garden gates to tulip fanatics. We find the divisions that flower most reliably over this late April timespan are Triumph (Division 3), Darwin Hybrids (Division 4), Single Late (Division 5), Lily-flowered (Division 6), Viridiflora (Division 8) and Double Late (Division 11). If the weather is unseasonably warm and dry, as we have experienced in recent years, the more portable containers can be stored in the shade to slow their progress and brought out in time for our scheduled open days.

When it comes to colour, I have developed a penchant for peaches and apricots, which surely must be a sign of growing older. Never did I think I would become obsessed with the subtle differences between 'Ollioules', 'Jimmy', 'Sanne' and 'Stunning Apricot'. Another colour range I am drawn to, which happens to work very well with the apricots, is black – never a true black, for no breeder has yet realized the goal of hybridizing a black tulip, but the very darkest of the blood-reds and deep purples on the market. I've experimented with many different shades and decided that 'Continental', a glossy, deep maroon Triumph, wins the prize for sheer depth of colour.

When creating combinations, it can be a good starting point to choose two different tulips in contrasting colours, such as apricot and black, then add two or three more cultivars for depth and subtlety. A container of 'Apricot Foxx' (a Triumph in tones of apricot and peach edged with pale tangerine) and the Single Late 'Café Noir' (a near-black chocolatey-maroon) will be enhanced by the addition of sweetly scented 'Brown Sugar' (another Triumph), pink-tinged 'Elegant Lady' (Lily-flowered) and perhaps a few stems of soft white 'Angels Wish' (another Single Late; see pp.180–1). It has long been considered bad taste to add white to a mix of coloured tulips, but I find that it can lift the arrangement and add an unexpected note. The joy of containers is that there are no rules – they are yours to experiment with, and if a combination really jars you can pick the offending stems to put in a vase or simply reassure yourself that they are a temporary aberration that will last for one season only.

Designing containers around contrasting colours is one option; creating tonal combinations, with different shades of one or two similar colours, is another. We have several large pots housing mixtures of greens and whites. One such combination (see p.242, bottom left) consists of the new introduction 'Antarctica Flame' (an ivory-white Triumph flamed with the palest yellow and a hint of green), Lily-flowered 'Sapporo' (palest yellow maturing to white, with a green central vein), 'Green King' (also sold as 'Evergreen', an unusual and long-lasting pure green) and the old favourite 'Spring Green' (both Viridiflora tulips). All these tulips are from divisions that adapt well to permanent planting schemes in the garden, so the bulbs can be lifted at the end of each season, dried and planted out to live a second life. In most containers there will be a minimum of two or three different forms of tulip, for I find that varying the heights, head shapes and leaves lends a pleasingly textured effect, particularly at scale. I have recently ordered a Coronet (Division 16) tulip called 'White Liberstar', which is bulbous at the base before nipping in at the waist and flaring out again at the tips of the petals, which roll in on themselves in a most unusual fashion. It will be added to one of our green-and-white mixtures for a touch of novelty, and I look forward to seeing whether any of our garden visitors recognize it as a Coronet, since the division was created only in 2018.

Sometimes I find myself creating container mixes that are subtle and sophisticated, yet lack bite. The sultry tones of the dark red Triumph tulips 'Paul Scherer' and 'Jan Reus', with the multi-headed Single Late 'Wallflower' added for good measure, make a good contrast with the majestic stark white French tulip 'Françoise' (another Triumph), but the result is frankly a little dull. Throw in the flamboyant red-and-yellow circus-striped 'Flaming Parrot' for some real exuberance, and the deadly serious historic 'Dom Pedro', and you will have a truly eclectic, layered combination (see p.185).

While tulips from many of the sixteen divisions work well planted in tandem, the doubles tend to be treated differently by dint of their shorter stems and heavier heads. We do sometimes combine doubles with their taller, more elegant cousins ('Black Hero', 'La Belle Époque' and 'Wyndham' work beautifully with Single Late and Triumph varieties), but as a rule we create sumptuous displays of both Double Early and Double Lates (Divisions 2 and 11) on a macro and micro scale. Antique cast-iron drain hoppers are filled with them, they flounce out of old-fashioned dolly tubs and metal containers in the walled garden (overleaf, 'Charming Lady', 'Foxy Foxtrot', 'Orange Princess', and 'Wyndham' is one of my favourite

combinations), and we have a massive steel planter (in fact an old cow trough) 1.2 m (4 ft) in diameter in which a tapestry effect is formed using eight or nine different cultivars in mottled shades of burgundy and bronze (see p.240, bottom left). Double tulips have received a bad press over the centuries – Daniel Hall famously wrote in 1929, 'The doubling of a flower is always a doubtful blessing, but to double a tulip is to destroy the finest and most distinctive qualities that it should possess' – but I love their full-blown peony-like ruffles, their ability to withstand wind and their extra-long flowering period. Having said all that, double tulips do struggle in persistent rain, and the complex structure of their petals means that they take longer to dry out than most single tulips, and so are prone to botrytis.

Limiting yourself to a single cultivar in a container is a good way to accommodate any impulse buys, trial new varieties or experiment with different divisions. Our tulip season at Blacklands is geared towards mid- to late-season divisions, but I play with early-flowering tulips by planting them in pots. Kaufmanniana Group tulips (Division 12) are some of the earliest to come into bloom, and cheer up a dull day when their wonderfully elongated petals open wide to the weakest of March sunshine. While they do not marry well with other divisions, a Kaufmanniana (or Waterlily type, as they are also known), such as 'Ice Stick' or 'Johann Strauss', looks sensational in a pot of its own. The pure white Lily-flowered tulip 'Très Chic' lives up to its name when planted a dozen at a time in a series of 23 cm (9 in) terracotta pots, ranked along a table. Single varieties in small pots are easily carried around the garden or brought for a few days into the house, where they can be observed at close quarters and their subtle scent appreciated. There is nothing more thrilling than watching the journey a tulip takes from simple bud through to full-blown inflorescence.

Since the mid-2010s it has become the vogue to plant container tulips in several layers, to create what is known as 'bulb lasagne' or 'tulip tiramisu'. While I have tried this and find it useful if planting a mixture of different genuses, such as tulips, *Narcissus* (daffodils) and *Muscari* (grape hyacinths), I prefer to plant a container consisting entirely of tulips in one densely packed layer, so that I can determine the pattern the different colours and forms will create. Most of our containers are composed solely of tulips, because that is my passion. Sometimes I add spring interest to the top layer of soil, such as a sprinkling of forget-me-nots (*Myosotis sylvatica*) or wallflowers (*Erysimum* spp.), a few cardoons for their spiky silver leaves or ferns for their evergreen ruffles (see opposite), but for the most part I like the tulips to put their shoots upwards and their roots downwards unhindered by other bulbs or plant material. I am in agreement with John Parkinson, who wrote in his *Paradisi in Sole Paradisus Terrestris* (1629) that 'if the seede lye one upon another, that it hath not roome upon the sprouting, to enter and take roote in the earth, it perisheth by and by'.

Container plantings provide the greatest opportunity for creative expression in the garden, since the schemes can be changed each year. I see them as an opportunity to paint pictures with flowers, playing with the different tones and textures in juxtaposition with one another. The enormous range of cultivars offers limitless flexibility and endless fun for the gardener who is willing to experiment.

A perennial planting in the rose garden, of *Tulipa* 'Black Hero' with
self-seeded wildflowers, such as the primrose (*Primula vulgaris*),
and hazel domes behind. Pages 192–3: *T.* 'Virichic', 'Request',
'Greenstar' and 'Black Hero' in the rose garden.

Perennial plantings with annual tulips

The perennial plantings at Blacklands are created with the intention that they will flower year on year, without ever having to be dug up or moved. This means no bulk purchases of bulbs for the borders each year (after the original order), no fiddly planting between perennial plants each year and no heavy lifting when flowering is over. Instead, the soil structure can be left virtually intact, bulb orders are reduced significantly and labour is saved with a no-mow approach (for those bulbs planted in grass) during the flowering period and for six to eight weeks afterwards.

Enduring, naturalistic displays can be formulated in both flower beds and areas of grass. There is no doubt that planting in beds is more straightforward – the bulbs can be packed in densely and there is no turf for them to compete with – but the effect achieved by dotting tulips through fresh spring grass is to my mind more desirable. We work with both settings throughout the garden, evaluating the success of the separate plantings each year. Our informal scoring system is based on the percentage of tulips that repeat-flower (this is an estimate – I don't count!), how they cope with the weather and the reaction of visitors. Whether the tulips appeal to my personal aesthetic is, of course, also a strong factor. What works in my garden may not work in yours, depending on soil type, aspect and other factors, so it is worth experimenting to see what suits.

We have made a conscious decision to plant only species tulips rather than cultivars in mixed herbaceous beds (see p.44), but we have allowed garden hybrids into the formal rose beds in the rose garden, and into the productive walled garden. We created initial shortlists bearing in mind colour combinations, variations in form and suitability for perennial planting. Minimal quantities were then ordered and trialled over a season in situ before the choices were tweaked as necessary and augmented for the following year. The rose garden now has a perennial display formed of four different cultivars, which are never lifted, repeat reliably and are supplemented with approximately 20–30 per cent new bulbs every year to guarantee a full display. If we didn't open the garden I would be tempted not to add any, but I don't want to disappoint people who are paying an entrance fee for charity.

Viridiflora and Lily-flowered cultivars are the tulips that perform best as perennials in our garden, and these are often the starting point for a new scheme. In the rose garden we chose 'Virichic' as the star of the show. This elegant fuchsia-pink variety has a strong flush of green on the reverse of the reflexed petals; the fact that it is a Viridiflora might explain its staying power (see overleaf and p.212). Its vibrant tones are cooled by the company of 'Greenstar', a Lily-flowered tulip, which is much like it in form but cream and green in colour, and a little finer. Among these grow a spattering of 'Request', a pointy-petalled Triumph in orange with a pink flame in the centre of each petal that has surprised us with its capacity to repeat-flower, and 'Black Hero', a peony-flowered Double Late version of 'Queen of Night' that has proven its worth as a perennial. 'Black Hero's' head is notably smaller after the first season, but I find this subtler version sits more comfortably in a garden setting, particularly since the roses are trained around hazel domes and provide an informal backdrop.

Top: In the walled garden in front of an established planting of *Paeonia daurica*
subsp. *mlokosewitschii* (Molly the Witch) is a wide band of two contrasting pale
tulips, 'Maureen' and 'City of Vancouver'; Above: The wildflower turf in front
of the house contains perennial plantings of *Tulipa* 'Claudia', 'Queen of Night',
'Menton', 'Spring Green', 'Marilyn' and 'Maytime'.

The walled garden is also the perfect setting for perennial tulip plantings, which punctuate the productive beds throughout the spring. The beds are free-draining and protected by high walls, and we have been able to play with combinations that don't rely on Lily-flowered or Viridiflora cultivars as their starting point. An equal mix of 'Havran', 'Disaronno' and 'Cairo' (all Triumph, see pp.6–7) has become a favourite early-flowering combination. 'Disaronno', a rich golden-yellow with a crimson interior and edges to the petals, is worth growing perennially not least because it is hard to obtain; 'Cairo' contrasts beautifully with its burnt-copper tones (see also p.197) and has the most bewitching scent that stops you in your tracks – but be prepared to top up its numbers each year, since it is not the most reliable repeat-flowerer. 'Havran' is the perfect foil, with tones of deepest claret and up to three flowers per stem. In another area, next to a dense row of *Paeonia daurica* subsp. *mlokosewitschii* (usually known for simplicity as 'Molly the Witch'), we have a thick strip of *Tulipa* 'Maureen' and 'City of Vancouver', whose cool tones work well with the lemon-yellow bowls of the peony. We are continually assessing trial combinations for their perennial qualities and to see how well they work with the medley of spring-flowering bulbs and plants that share the space: *Helleborus* 'Slaty Blue' and various Harvington hybrids, *Narcissus* 'Thalia' beneath the eaves of the greenhouse, rows of *Muscari armeniacum* tucked under stepover apple trees, and the demure blossoms of goblet-trained pears (*Pyrus* spp.).

Outside the confines of the walled garden we have managed to naturalize hybrid tulips successfully in grass, primarily in front of the house in stretches of wildflower turf beneath a square of pollarded lime trees (*Tilia × europaea* 'Pallida'), and either side of the back drive as you enter the confines of the garden and are welcomed by an established planting of joyful perennial tulips (see pp.214–15). Here the tulips are less protected from the Wiltshire weather and must compete with a well-established sward, so we make careful choices when we plan a perennial planting. Should you wish to expand your options beyond the reliably repeating Lily-flowered and Viridifloras, I recommend choosing from divisions that include hybrids with a strong injection of wild, species tulips: 12 (Kaufmanniana), 13 (Fosteriana) and 14 (Greigii). The pure-white 'Purissima' (syn. 'White Emperor') and its pink-flushed sport 'Flaming Purissima' are excellent Fosteriana choices, which flower early and last for weeks. Be aware that they start out a strong creamy yellow, which fades to a white base colour as they mature (I thought I had received the wrong bulbs when I planted them the first time). The wide grass strip alongside our back drive has a strong representation of tulips from these divisions, providing endless pleasure as they flower over a whole month, even six weeks. Kaufmannianas and Greigiis can be wonderful in a rockery or crevice garden, but sadly they don't fit easily into our naturalized settings at Blacklands. A trial of 'Ice Stick' (Kaufmanniana) and 'Serano' (Greigii) was promising from the endurance point of view, but they were too short to work visually with the established schemes and have now been consigned to containers.

Darwin Hybrids also have a significant species component in their make-up, being a cross between species tulips (most often *T. fosteriana*) and the old Krelage Darwins. We keep returning to the blush-pink 'Mystic van Eijk', as well as 'Ivory Floradale', both late-flowering with enormous heads that seem to hold on to their petals whatever the weather. 'Light and Dreamy' challenged me initially (see p.197 on the right and p.247, in the foreground) – mauve isn't normally on my radar as a tulip colour – but its ethereal tones grew on me and it has now found a permanent place in the rough grass towards the compost heaps. 'Ollioules' is the prettiest pink I grow (across all applications – naturalized, in containers and for cutting) and worth ordering early before it sells out.

Triumphs are the last group we select from extensively for perennial displays. We have had particularly strong results with 'Jimmy' and 'Request', and we plan to plant 'Mistress Mystic' among the cardoons in the walled garden. Don't, however, be afraid of experimenting with hybrids from other divisions; you will always get one year's worth of good flowering from your purchase even if the subsequent years are disappointing. We have a handful of Single Lates that have returned our initial investment many times over, including the stately French tulip 'Menton', which – despite being arguably too tall for its situation – glows iridescently in the spring grass in front of the house, and historic 'Dom Pedro', which provides a touch of gravitas beside the back drive. 'Black Parrot' (Division 10) is a stalwart that keeps coming back, but it is the only Parrot tulip I trust to do so.

It is no matter of chance that these curated displays look good every year. But on the opposite verge of the back drive, leading to the firepit and compost bays, is a medley of rejected and recycled hybrid tulips (see pp.4–5 and p.244). Leftovers from part-used bags are thrown in alongside misorders, old bulbs that have lost their labels and oddities that just don't belong anywhere else. The area is left unweeded and untended, and the tulips jostle for space among a hotchpotch of other spring bulbs that have been grown in containers and planted out: hyacinths and jonquils, grape hyacinths and fritillaries. Tall stems of cow parsley tower over the array of bulbs beneath and help to soften the effect, but don't quite manage to make it tasteful. Suffice to say that every single person who visits in springtime says that this entirely accidental perennial planting is their favourite part of the garden. I am secretly in agreement.

Annual tulips for cutting

Home-grown hybrid tulips are the ultimate cut flower. Dry, dormant bulbs planted in the depths of winter will produce flowers the following spring that can have stems over 75 cm (30 in) in length, come in quite literally thousands of colourways, and be classically simple, joyfully multi-headed or thrillingly pointy-petalled, with every variation of form in between. Once cut, a tulip will not only last for weeks in the vase but also keep growing, becoming more and more sinuous as it morphs on its journey from bud to full-blown bloom. A tulip even looks beautiful – some would say most beautiful – in its dying days as it gracefully drops its petals one by one.

If you intend to pick tulips to arrange in the house, it is a good idea to grow a selection in a designated area, so that you are not constantly pillaging the garden. Incorporating a few rows of hybrid tulips in a vegetable garden or allotment is very straightforward, since the flowers can be cut freely and the bulbs lifted and replaced with edible or ornamental summer crops. If you are growing at scale to supply private or wholesale customers, it is worth investing in infrastructure that is fenced off and ideally has enough space for you to rotate your tulips each year (see pp.198–9). Planting tulips repeatedly in the same position can deplete the soil and allow pathogens, such as tulip fire or eelworm, to establish.

At Blacklands, we grow tulips for cutting in a separate flower field away from the main garden, protected against deer and rabbits with a mesh fence 1.8 m (6 ft) tall and an additional barrier of windproofed screening. The set-up is agricultural in nature and not focused on appearance (although it is actually quite pretty). Over the past decade we have established a system that works well. Lines of equal-sized beds have been cut out of the turf, with woodchip paths running between them and a tap for irrigation at the end of alternate rows. Tulips are planted in a different portion of the field each year, on a four-year rotation, so that the soil in each area is free of tulips for three years before being populated once again. In the intervening years dahlias and annual flowers for cutting are cropped, a few vegetables are grown and a green manure is sown over the winter months. The ethos is to feed back into the soil by planting a continuous and diverse range of plants, to provide a wide spectrum of nutrients that will ultimately benefit the tulips. Keeping a constant ground cover has the additional benefit of protecting the soil structure and capturing carbon from the atmosphere, which is something that should be considered in this time of climate change.

I have cut down considerably on the quantities of tulips that I grow for cutting, compared to the early days of my business, because my earlier approach no longer aligns with the environmental ethos I follow. Still, I purchase and plant several thousand each year. I would love to say that all our bulbs are organic, but the reality is that there are relatively few organic varieties on the market, and those that are available are considerably more expensive than the non-organic ones. For now, I have decided to buy as many Soil Association-certified organic bulbs (in the United States, this would be those with Organic Certification and Accreditation) as possible, and supplement them with orders from mainstream wholesale merchants. There is no doubt that producing tulips for the cut-flower industry presents me with an ethical conundrum. I do not feel entirely comfortable with the fact that I am purchasing quantities of bulbs that have been chemically grown and treated before they reach me, but at the same time I know that it is better for the environment if I can supply clients with top-quality tulips that have been grown outside to organic standards, and produced locally. No pesticides, fungicides or artificial fertilizers are applied once the bulbs come into our custodianship, and no air miles are incurred. The alternative is for customers to buy cut tulips that are supplied by large-scale producers, where they will have been grown hydroponically, sprayed with chemicals and kept at a constant heat under glass or plastic, and will have incurred significant air or road miles on their route to market.

The quality and size of the tulips grown by us and other small-scale flower farms put them in a different league from tulips that are grown on an industrial scale, and they are considerably fresher and last longer as a result. Commercial crops are cut while they are still tightly in bud, so they can be transported easily without damage to the petals. They spend prolonged periods out of water and are kept refrigerated, all the while arguably losing precious days of their lives. Our tulips are cut only when they are fully ripe, still just about in bud but showing colour, meaning that their full potential is realized in terms of stem length, head size and that subtle scent that you only ever get with home-grown tulips. They are cut to order, conditioned in the cool of our coach house, with no need for refrigeration, and transported in water after leaving us, so there is continuity of care. The time it takes for them to go from field to final destination is less than twenty-four hours, and this is reflected in their longevity in the vase.

Picking tulips in the flower field. Seen here are the red-and-yellow
Tulipa 'Flaming Parrot' and pinkish 'Apricot Parrot'.

A wild arrangement in tones of bruised lilac and purple, using the
historic tulips 'Bleu Aimable' and 'La Joyeuse', *Iris* 'Benton Deidre',
intersectional peonies, *Nectaroscordum siculum* and ranunculus.

I believe you should grow whatever you please for cutting, although such factors as the aspect of your site should certainly be taken into account. If Parrot tulips are your passion, for example, you will have to grow them in a sheltered position, since their heavy heads are vulnerable to wind damage. For that reason I have whittled my Parrot tulips for cutting down to 'Black Parrot' and 'Apricot Parrot', the most robust (having been tempted by other cultivars, such as 'Blumex Favourite' and 'Rasta Parrot', whose heads had an alarming tendency to snap off overnight). Soil is a consideration, as it always should be with tulips. It doesn't have to be perfect – an annual crop for cutting needs to survive for only one year, since the bulbs aren't recycled – but if it is heavy clay there is a risk that the bulbs will rot before spring arrives. Ours is alluvial and quite free-draining, but if yours is on the heavier side with a high clay content, mix in some horticultural sand and strive to improve the soil structure in the long term by adding organic matter regularly, outside the growing season.

Rather than choosing ad hoc from catalogues when they arrive, create a plan that spans the whole spring, so that you will have tulips for cutting from the tail end of March until the beginning of May, without a glut during one particular period. Some bulb companies list tulips by division, which is helpful because you can target the Fosteriana, Single Early and Double Early sections for the start of the season, followed by Triumphs, Viridifloras and Darwin Hybrids for mid-season flowering. Single and Double Lates and Parrots will then take you through into May. Beyond the timings – which admittedly go haywire during a long, hot, dry spring, when all the tulips will decide to flower at the same time – it is worth dipping into a selection of different divisions to get a variety of forms. I am passionate about Lily-flowered varieties and quite the opposite about Fringed ones (Division 7), although I have a penchant for one of those, 'Bastia', a golden-yellow tulip edged in carmine, with green flames up the central veins of the petals. It manages to be fringed, double and viridiflora all at the same time and is quite magnificent for it.

Pick out colours that you love, in varying tones, and challenge yourself with the occasional colour that you don't think you love. No two 'blacks' are exactly the same, and in my opinion you can never grow enough of these dramatic tulips; you will appreciate every single stem you pick of 'Continental', 'Blackjack' (a Triumph), 'Café Noir' and 'Black Hero'. Throw in a lilac, too, perhaps the newly bred lavender-hued Triumph 'Lilac Love' or the distinctly purple Double Late 'Lilac Perfection'. I am not keen on purple as a rule, but I recognize that it is good to be pushed out of my comfort zone and I can be sure that one of my customers will have a sudden, last-minute call for the colour.

Whites are always in demand, and we grow a wide selection in different shapes that flower at different times. Lily-flowered varieties include the vestal white 'Très Chic' and buttery 'Sapporo', a little later to flower and more slender in form. Add to those the elegant 'Purissima', 'Ivory Floradale' (with huge egg shaped ivory flowers) and the peony-flowered Double Late 'Mount Tacoma' and you will be well covered.

I always try to have a representation of classic, traditional tulips, those garden hybrids that have endured the test of time because they are simply so beautiful and dependable that you can't live without them. French tulips (not actually French, but often named after French towns or regions) were first bred in the 1960s from 'Mrs John T. Scheepers' and belong in the Single Late division. Stems are exceptionally long (well over 75 cm/30 in if you pull them attached to the bulb) and strong, too, able to weather gales and stand tall throughout their lengthy flowering period. It has been discovered that they contain extra chromosomes, which explains this robustness. Foliage is neat, and the leaves add to their impact in the vase, but it is their chalice-shaped heads and strength of colour that draw me and other admirers to them: 'Menton', in deepest rose-pink and coral, 'Dordogne', in saturated baby-pink and tangerine, and 'Avignon', standing proud in startling red softened at the edges of the petals with fine brushes of apricot. Even pure white 'Maureen' seems infused with extra pigment, giving it added presence in the ground or the vase. French tulips can work well as perennials, too, but most are rather too tall for our naturalized schemes at Blacklands and stand out from the crowd in the wrong way.

Not as majestic in scale, but equally deserving of their place in the cutting field, are such mid-twentieth-century classics as the burnished copper 'Prinses Irene', a bowl-shaped Triumph streaked with burgundy up the centre of each petal, and 'Artist', a Viridiflora in dramatic orange-gold and green. 'Abu Hassan' is an excellent mid-season Triumph in deep red with golden-yellow edges. None of these has a place in our Dutch Historic collection (see Chapter 2), because they are in continuous supply and far from rare, but they are tulips that deserve to be revered.

Less reverential are a host of hybrid tulips that must be grown for the sheer joy and exuberance they bring to house and garden. They look somewhat incongruous when growing in rows outside against bare soil, but cut, conditioned and arranged they deservedly become the centre of attention. 'Estella Rijnveld' is a scarlet-and-white-striped Parrot; she has been shouting for attention ever since her introduction in 1954, and is best not ignored. If you prefer something a little quieter or softer, consider 'Sorbet', a Single Late in shades of white streaked with a faded raspberry pink, or the relatively recent Triumph introduction of pillar-box red and white called 'Happy Generation', a single version of the dense peony-flowered 'Carnaval de Nice'. Sometimes classed as Rembrandts, these do not in fact belong in that division (Division 9) and are nothing like the old broken Rembrandt tulips that live in our historic collection, but they are fabulous when grown as cut flowers and you will never find anything like them in a flower shop.

Organizing tulip bulbs in cutting beds presents a good opportunity to play with the colour spectrum. You could plant them at random, for a multicoloured barcode effect, or give the positioning careful consideration, placing similar tones alongside one another in the style of a paint chart (see pp.206–207). The latter approach is handy for comparing variations of the same colour range. I start by allocating beds for Singles, Doubles and Parrots, so that I can view the range of tulips as a whole; a modest block of fifty or so doubles will disappear from view if planted between two sections of tall Single Lates. Huddled together a long run of different doubles creates a satisfying ripple of ruffled petals, and means they are not overshadowed by their taller cousins. The next stage is to subdivide into colour ranges. Starting with blacks, we progress through browns and bronzes to burnt oranges, apricots and pinks (with the occasional purple imposter), slipping in bicolours where they fit best. I try to create an ombré effect along a bed, which is most pleasing to the eye – until a mis-supply of pillar-box red rears its head among the whites and the effect is ruined. The wildcard always brings a smile to my face, though, and confirms that in the business of growing plants – even intensively hybridized tulips – we are never truly in control of nature.

A large-scale arrangement in an enamelled tin bucket for a National
Garden Scheme open day, including *Tulipa* 'Danceline', 'Sanne',
'Vincent van Gogh', 'Apricot Parrot' and 'Flaming Parrot'.

Simple steps to planting tulips in containers, showing crocks,
spacing of bulbs and top-dressing with fine gravel.

Growing Annual Tulips in Containers

As with species tulips (see p.89), we start planting our annual tulips in containers in November. Always put crocks in the base of the container, to prevent soil or roots from clogging up the drainage holes; we use shards of broken terracotta or chunks of old polystyrene packaging, which are recycled year on year. To aid drainage further, place large containers on terracotta feet or discreetly hidden strips of wood, so that excess rain can flow freely out of the bottom of the container and prevent waterlogging. Plant the bulbs at a depth of about 10 cm (4 in) regardless of their size – they will be dug up soon after flowering and replaced with summer displays, so there is little point in planting them more deeply. They can be placed so close together that they almost touch, leaving just a fraction of soil between them to prevent rotting. Once the soil has been added, top-dress small pots with a 5 mm (¼ in) layer of grit to give them a pleasing finish and deter snails, and this helps with drainage too (as well as preventing splashback from watering). It is neither practical nor attractive to add a layer of grit to larger containers.

In some of the most prominent containers in the walled garden, such as those flanking the entrance to the greenhouse, I incorporate Dutch Historic tulips. These super-special bulbs (see Chapter 2) are planted individually in small aquatic pots (which provide good drainage), to keep them from becoming mixed up with the annual bulbs. Each pot has a label placed at the bottom of it, so that the bulb is readily identified when the display is taken apart after flowering. It can then be dried out separately for future plantings.

The quality of the soil used in containers is important if you plan to recycle the tulips for perennial plantings, since they require plenty of goodness to bulk up for the subsequent season. We make up a fresh mix every year, consisting of equal quantities of our own (already very free-draining) topsoil, a peat-free multipurpose compost and sharp sand (otherwise known as horticultural sand). In the early days of my tulip journey, when we simply composted most of the bulbs after they had flowered, we would use a multipurpose compost with nothing added. This is a perfectly acceptable option, but there is no doubt that a handful or two of sand or grit improves drainage and is beneficial over the mild, wet winters that we are beginning to experience. When the containers are emptied after the tulips have flowered, the spent soil is added to the compost bays to continue the cycle of life.

Some of our containers are truly outsize, and these are planted in situ since there is no hope of moving them once they are full of soil. Dolly tubs are lined up in the service yard for planting, and later wheeled out across the garden as the tulips come into bud, whereas smaller pots are stored behind cold frames for protection from the worst of the elements until they are moved to their final flowering place. Every container we plant is immediately protected against squirrels, which are enemy number one; chicken wire moulded into conical 'hats' is the most effective option, but I do like the appearance of short lengths of prickly holly plunged into the soil, a trick I learned from Matt Collins, head gardener at the Garden Museum in London. Another tried-and-tested option is to sprinkle chilli powder or flakes liberally over the surface of the soil; this is effective against squirrels so long as it is replaced at regular intervals, for it loses potency over time, particularly during rainy periods. Mice are best kept at bay with traps strategically placed and baited with chocolate, although we don't have much of a problem with them at Blacklands. Our head gardener, Andy Wilson, is experimenting with sonar deterrents, and the signs are good. My suspicion is that the mice are confounded by the sheer quantity of bulbs they are faced with – or perhaps I simply don't notice when a bulb or two goes missing.

Irrigation is a question we debate every year: to water or not to water the containers as soon as they have been planted? I tend not to, since the planting medium has plenty of moisture in it already; also, it usually rains within a short time and so the question answers itself. The containers are left undisturbed, rodent protection checked regularly, until the shoots are about 5–8 cm (2–3 in) high. At this point their defences can be removed, so that they don't damage and mark the leaves. After this the squirrels show no interest in the bulbs, turning their attention to other parts of the garden.

Once the tulips have come into bud we begin to feed them bi-weekly with an organic, diluted seaweed feed until flowering is in full swing. If it is a wet spring there will be little need for further irrigation, although over the past few years it has become increasingly necessary to water regularly as we experience unseasonably dry periods owing to climate change. Small containers dry out quickly, but larger ones can hold on to a surprising amount of water and are easily over-watered (dolly tubs being the worst culprit, because of their bulging shape, which encourages water retention). Always feel a couple of inches beneath the soil surface of each pot before watering, to check the moisture, and again afterwards, since the surface can appear wet but the water may not have penetrated far. One good watering a week is preferable to several scant ones, which will penetrate only the top layer of the soil rather than reaching the bulbs' roots. Always position the spout of the watering can at the edge of the pot, in order to reach underneath the dense layer of tulip leaves and prevent splash marks (or staining if there is feed in the water). Watering containers continues throughout the flowering period and is one of my favourite activities, since it affords the opportunity to assess and appreciate each individual variety of tulip and to evaluate the success (or failure) of new combinations.

Plant health is rarely a problem with container-grown tulips, since the bulbs are bought in afresh each year and the soil replaced. The dreaded tulip fire is generally unable to get a hold on these annuals, and the odd case of grey mould (*Botrytis cinerea*, characterized by weak stems, pale flowers and leaves) can be dealt with by carefully removing the entire plant, bulb and all. This unsightly fungus is usually caused by a damaged bulb becoming infected, so it is important to exercise quality control at the time of planting and discard any specimens that

are less than perfect. If you have trouble with slugs, you can remove them manually – taking extra care to check under the rim of each container – and scatter organically-approved slug pellets beneath the leaves at regular intervals.

More of a risk than disease is the discovery that some tulips will turn out to be entirely different from the ones that you selected and ordered so carefully. In an industry where billions of bulbs are produced every year, mix-ups are inevitable – particularly given that dormant bulbs are almost impossible to tell apart – but some companies are certainly more culpable than others. At the back of the book is a list of recommended suppliers (see p.255), which rarely mis-supply and are quick to rectify mistakes. Carefully ticking off deliveries against your original invoice is a good habit to get into, although even that is no guarantee that all surprises will be eliminated. This is where ordering unfashionable tulips can help, as you will be less likely to get substitutions.

Once flowering is over we deadhead the tulips in situ so they don't put their energy into producing seed heads, then leave them in their containers until we are ready for the big clear-out in mid- or late May. In an ideal world we wouldn't lift them until the leaves had browned and started to wither, but a garden full of dead container tulips is not a thing of beauty and we are always eager to start composing our summer arrangements. The tulips are dug up gently by hand and stored in racks in the yard, under cover but in the fresh air, where the bulbs will carry on absorbing nutrients as the leaves and stems die back. The cycle starts anew in November, when the bulbs are freed from the piles of desiccated leaves, ready to be planted as perennials or given away.

Trialling different dolly tub combinations against the backdrop
of the coach house – every year we experiment with different mixes.

Growing Annual Tulips as Perennials

The carefully designed perennial areas are initially planted with newly purchased bulbs, so that we can get an accurate sense of how the colours and forms work together, but they are thereafter supplemented with carefully edited bulbs recycled from containers, choosing only the largest ones that have not fragmented into bulblets. Some of the hybrids start to increase within a season or two, others take a few years, some dwindle away to nothing. We do not try to replace the dwindlers – it is a worthless exercise – but we do supplement those that are slow to establish with small quantities of new bulbs each season. The mixture of large, loud first-year bulbs and smaller, quieter naturalized ones creates an interesting textural effect and adds to the appeal; it is the complete opposite of a traditional bedding display, where homogeneous hybrid tulips are planted in symmetrical patterns as one-season wonders.

On the basis that these perennial tulips are expected to survive in the ground all year, we are comfortable planting them in late October, rather than holding off until colder weather arrives in November or December. It helps that our soil is free-draining; if you garden on clay you will have your work cut out with perennial tulip plantings, because your bulbs will be much more likely to rot in the ground.

There are a few tried-and-tested methods of making a planting look natural – throwing the bulbs and planting them where they land is the best-known – but I like to mix the various cultivars in a large trug and then dot them around, some huddled in clumps, others in isolation, in a seemingly haphazard but completely contrived fashion. Fergus Garrett, head gardener and steward of Christopher Lloyd's famous garden at Great Dixter in East Sussex, describes this aptly as 'high-density low-density planting'. A small, sharp 'lady's' spade can be used to slice a planting hole in the turf, but I prefer a bulb-planter. A scoop of sand poured into the base of each hole is recommended to prevent the bulb from sitting on wet soil and rotting, but I can't say I always do that with large plantings of annual tulips. We plant deep (15–20 cm/6–8 in) to confound the squirrels and protect the bulbs from extremes of temperature and possibly also from tulip fire, although more recent thinking suggests that shallow planting leads to higher survival rates and better naturalization. Time for another trial.

There should never be a need to water bulbs that are naturalized in grass, since the sward helps to retain moisture in the soil, but in recent years we have had to water perennial plantings in the garden borders and beds. When it comes to feeding, perennial tulips in grass are ignored whereas those in the rose beds and walled garden are included in the feeding rota and get a dose or two of a dilute organic seaweed feed before they come into flower, and once after flowering has finished. I am fastidious about picking up fallen petals, a practice that prevents botrytis (grey mould) from forming at the base of the plant. I can be seen tiptoeing daintily through the tulips throughout the months of April and May. Deadheading is highly recommended to encourage nutrients back into the creation of a new bulb, rather than the formation of energy-sapping seed heads, but in perennial plantings care must be taken not to tread on those flowers that are still in full bloom. Once the display is over naturalized tulips can be left to die back gracefully, the spring grass and weeds growing up to hide the decaying leaves and stems from view until the area is mown or strimmed six to eight weeks later, usually in the middle or end of June. In beds, other plants soon grow up to disguise the spent tulips, and we do some clearing once the brown stems and leaves can be pulled away with no resistance.

Growing Annual Tulips for Cutting

Planting tulips for cutting as an annual crop is a simple exercise that should be undertaken when autumn has turned into winter and there is a nip in the air. Beds can be at ground level or raised to improve drainage. Our cutting beds were cut straight out of turf and all measure 90 cm (35 in) across, the ideal width to reach across when planting bulbs (it is also just about possible to leap over the beds when they are empty, as a shortcut across the field). Other growers prefer to work with narrow trenches, 30 cm (12 in) or so wide, so that the harvesting can be executed from one side.

When digging trenches, choose a day when the ground is frost-free and workable, heaping all the soil to one side on a groundsheet. The depth of the trench will vary according to your soil; if it is loamy and free-draining you can dig a trench as shallow as 10–15 cm (4–6 in) and lay your bulbs straight on to the exposed surface, but if your soil is heavier, dig a deeper trench and add a 5 cm (2 in) raked layer of horticultural sand for the bulbs to sit on. This will keep their bases dry and minimize the risk of rot. I have experimented with planting bulbs for cutting at greater depths of 15–20 cm (6–8 in), but found it a challenge to lift the tulips with the bulbs intact. They invariably snapped off, incurring the loss of precious extra lengths of stem buried underground, and meaning that the bulbs had to be extracted separately, creating more work.

If you find that your soil is horribly difficult to work, with a high clay content, incorporate more sand into the backfilled mix, up to a third by volume. This will make a real difference to the soil structure and you will be grateful for it in years to come. If it is virtually unworkable, or space is short, consider growing your tulips for cutting in crates using a multipurpose potting compost. I know this method has been used successfully by some flower farmers, who have stopped trenching altogether.

At Blacklands, we like the bulbs to be in straight lines, with both rows and bulbs spaced about 5–8 cm (2–3 in) apart. Some growers plant theirs cheek by jowl like eggs in an egg box, so that they are practically touching (as you would in a container planting), but we have plenty of space in our field and prefer to let air circulate for optimum plant health. Exercise quality control as you go, and if a bulb feels less than firm or has a bloom of mould, discard it.

With luck, your newly planted bulbs will be safe against attack from squirrels or mice, which seem to prefer their bulbs conveniently served in containers, rather than digging for them in open ground. Covering the rows with netting stretched between hoops will deter squirrels if they are a problem, and has the added benefit of protecting the flowers against hailstorms (which are a hazard for the darker tulips in particular). Clear plastic is an option, but we do not use it since it is not in line with our environmental ethos. In any case, it can bring the flowers on too quickly, starves them of rainwater and makes the harvesting procedure tricky – I have ended up crawling commando-style up the rows under low arches of plastic. Not a good look. Fine netting is our preferred option, since it provides a little shade, doesn't heat the tulips up too much and can be reused year after year.

Labelling is possibly the most important part of the whole planting process. Immediately after covering the bulbs, label each separate row or block (depending on quantities) fastidiously using indelible pen. Nothing is more frustrating than not being able to identify a tulip, and it will inevitably be the one you haven't grown before and don't recognize. A quick sketch showing what you have planted where is always useful; we have a map of the field that I mark up annually and also use to chart the rotation of the beds.

As with container tulips, there is generally no need to water upon planting, but we have had to irrigate a few times during the growing period over the past few years given the lack of spring rainfall. Dilute liquid fertilizer (an organic seaweed feed) is administered by watering can when the tips of the tulips are a couple of inches out of the ground, and every two weeks thereafter. Do take care to water from underneath once the flowers are fully in bud, as the feed can stain the petals. Weeds will not be rampant at this time of year, which is a relief, so the onus is on feeding and harvesting the flowers when they are ready. Diseases among tulips grown as annuals are few and far between, and mitigated by rotating the beds each year. If any tulip looks suspicious – spots on the foliage or petals, grey mildew, contorted flower head – it should be dug out carefully and burned, ensuring that it doesn't touch and contaminate its neighbours in the process. Given our organic status, this is the only approach we can take.

A major benefit of growing cut flowers at home is that the tulips can reach their full potential in the ground before being harvested, so wait as long as possible to reap the rewards of extra stem length and head size. To extract the whole tulip from the soil, place both hands a few inches apart (the lower one at the bottom of the stem just above the basal leaves) and pull firmly at an angle, taking care that your back doesn't give (I speak from experience). In theory the plant should come out with the bulb still attached, although they do have a maddening habit of snapping off. After extracting the whole tulip, cut off the bulb with secateurs, strip off the large lower leaves and put the tulip straight into a bucket containing a couple of inches of clean water. I use old metal buckets for conditioning and storing the tulips, since they are a pleasure to work with as well as looking more pleasing than stacks of plastic ones. The tulips are left to have a good drink in the cool of my workshop for at least twelve hours before they wend their way to their new homes. I don't wrap them in newspaper, as some florists suggest, to keep their stems poker-straight, because they don't stay with me for long – and if they should start to twist and turn, so be it. They are a natural product and should look that way.

Clockwise from top left: Annual tulips are pulled from the cutting field with their bulbs intact; conditioning cut flowers in the coach house, where they sit overnight; stripping the leaves from annual tulips before they are conditioned in buckets of fresh, cold water (see pp.220–221); hand-tied bunches for sale at a charity open day (see pp.186–87).

SINGLE EARLY

DOUBLE EARLY

TRIUMPH

DARWIN HYBRIDS

SINGLE LATE

LILY-FLOWERED

FRINGED

VIRIDIFLORA

REMBRANDT

PARROT

DOUBLE LATE

KAUFMANNIANA GROUP

FOSTERIANA GROUP

GREIGII GROUP

MISCELLANEOUS

CORONET

Tulips are currently classified in sixteen divisions, which are revised periodically. Each division is given a number and a name; in this book I have chosen on the whole to use the name, since it is more descriptive of the tulips than a number, and hence easier to remember. The list of divisions starts with the early-flowering Single Early (Division 1) varieties and works its way through the flowering season to Double Late (Division 11), with tulips of different forms, such as Lily-flowered and Parrot, placed in between. Those in which the imprint of wild tulips is most evident are placed in Divisions 12–14, while the pure species (botanical) tulips and their cultivars are termed Miscellaneous (Division 15). A new, smaller division called Coronet was added in 2018 at the end, as Division 16. There are many thousands of tulip cultivars, and more are becoming available all the time. The tulips named as 'Best for containers' and so on in this section of the book are those I grow and love, rather than a comprehensive list of cultivars in each division. Note that Hortus Bulborum has its own system of divisions, which does not exactly follow those of the RHS or KAVB.

DIVISION 1

SINGLE EARLY

Early-flowering

Best for containers
ALL DUC VAN TOL CULTIVARS,
'KEIZERSKROON'

Best for perennial planting
NONE AT BLACKLANDS

Best for cutting
'APRICOT BEAUTY' |↗|,
'CANDY PRINCE', 'GENERAAL
DE WET'

Single Early tulips are among the first to flower, in late March and early April, with a neat form of attractive cup-shaped flowers on short stems. They were originally created as a result of crossing two species, *Tulipa schrenkii* (also known as *T. suaveolens*) and *T. gesneriana*, and are traditionally forced for the cut-flower industry or used as bedding plants. At Blacklands we do neither of these, rather growing Single Earlies in containers to dot around the garden – focusing on the historic Duc van Tol cultivars (see p.130) – and in the flower field for cutting. They are my first proper tulip crop of the year. As a result of their short stature, they withstand most bad weather, although they can fall victim to hailstorms, when their sizeable petals become ruined by pockmarks.

DIVISION 2

DOUBLE EARLY

Early-flowering

Best for containers
'BROWNIE', 'LA BELLE ÉPOQUE',
'NACHTWACHT'

Best for perennial planting
NONE AT BLACKLANDS

Best for cutting
'FOXY FOXTROT', 'GERARD DOU' ⟋,
'GLOBAL DESIRE', 'MONDIAL',
'VERONA'

Also known as Peony tulips (as are their later-flowering cousins the Double Lates), these have bowl-shaped flower heads, dense with petals that often obscure the centres completely. They are frequently described as untidy or muddled, but I am drawn to their heavily textured appearance and early flowering. Stems are shortish, helping to support the heads and giving them longevity – they last for weeks in containers and the cutting field. This is an excellent cut flower, often with a light subtle scent, that lends itself to forcing on a commercial scale.

DIVISION 3

TRIUMPH

Mid-season

Best for containers
'ANTARCTICA FLAME', 'APRICOT FOXX', 'BROWN SUGAR', 'CARNAVAL DE RIO', 'GAVOTA', 'JAN REUS', 'SANNE'

Best for perennial planting
'CAIRO', 'JIMMY', 'MISTRESS MYSTIC', 'REQUEST', 'RONALDO' ⊠, 'SHIRLEY'

Best for cutting
'ABU HASSAN', 'ALEXANDER PUSHKIN', 'CONTINENTAL', 'HAPPY GENERATION', 'PRINSES IRENE'

This is the largest and most adaptable division, with tulips that lend themselves to most applications: forcing, cutting, containers and perennializing. Triumphs fill the gap between early- and late-flowering varieties (unless there is a heatwave, in which case most of the divisions will try to flower at the same time). Long-stemmed with large flowers in an enormous array of tones, many are bicoloured with tinted borders or contrasting splashes of colour. They are the result of hybridization between Single Earlies, old Krelage Darwins (see Division 5, p.228) and old breeder tulips.

DIVISION 4

DARWIN HYBRIDS
Mid-season

Best for containers
'APRICOT IMPRESSION',
'OLLIOULES'

Best for perennial planting
'IVORY FLORADALE', 'LIGHT
AND DREAMY', 'MYSTIC VAN EIJK'

Best for cutting
'DESIGN IMPRESSION',
'GUDOSHNIK' [↗], 'SALMON
VAN EIJK'

Darwin Hybrids are extraordinarily tall, reaching 70 cm (28 in) and considerably more if they are lifted with the bulbs still attached, which can add a good 15 cm (6 in) of extra stem that was previously hidden in the soil. With single, huge flowers of a slightly tapering classic tulip shape, they are the product of hybridizing species tulips (most notably *T. fosteriana*) with Krelage Darwins and cultivars from the Single Early and Triumph divisions. The injection of species has resulted in tulips with good perennial properties, such as 'Apeldoorn', which can thrive for decades in a garden setting – as I found out when we inherited clumps of both the red and yellow varieties at Blacklands. Be warned that some cultivars, such as 'Ivory Floradale', which opens to a generous bowl shape, can look overblown in a perennial planting scheme if you include too many of them.

SINGLE LATE

Late-flowering

Best for containers
'ANGELS WISH', 'BLEU AIMABLE',
'STUNNING APRICOT'

Best for perennial planting
'DOM PEDRO', 'MENTON' [↗],
'QUEEN OF NIGHT'

Best for cutting
'AVIGNON', 'BLUSHING GIRL',
'DORDOGNE', 'EL NINO',
'MAUREEN', 'SORBET'

With its super-long, strong stems of up to 70 cm (28 in) and perfect cup-shaped flowers in painterly shades, this division contains some of my favourite tulips for containers and cutting. The division (created in 1981) is largely constituted of the old Darwins bred by E. H. Krelage at the end of the nineteenth century, Cottage tulips rescued from old English gardens, and hybrids of the two. The fashionable French tulips, such as 'Avignon' and 'Françoise', belong here. Single Lates have traditionally been grown as bedding tulips, for which their height and staying power are unrivalled, but since we don't do bedding schemes at Blacklands I like to try to perennialize a few. So far we have been successful with 'Dom Pedro' (one of our Dutch Historic tulips; see p.111), 'Queen of Night' and 'Menton'.

DIVISION 6

LILY-FLOWERED

Late-flowering

Best for containers
'BALLADE', 'ELEGANT LADY', 'FLY AWAY', 'GREENSTAR', 'MAYTIME'

Best for perennial planting
'BALLERINA', 'BURGUNDY' [↗], 'MARILYN', 'WHITE TRIUMPHATOR'

Best for cutting
'SAPPORO', 'STRIKING MATCH', 'TRÈS CHIC'

Pointy-petalled, elegantly waisted tulips that often reflex outwards at their tips. The first successful hybridization to produce a Lily-flowered tulip was between the Cottage tulip 'Retroflexa' and the old Krelage Darwin 'Psyche', resulting in the satiny pink 'Sirene', which caused a sensation when it was launched in 1910. 'Sirene' is no longer in existence, but there is a fantastic range of Lily-flowered tulips to choose from, many of them viridiflora with brushstrokes of green on the backs of the petals, and others bicoloured. Tulips in this division have strong perennial properties, and I frequently use them in containers for a year before adding them to permanent planting schemes in the garden. Having become increasingly popular in the 1940s, they were assigned their own division in 1958.

DIVISION 7

FRINGED

Late-flowering

Best for containers
'BASTIA', 'BURGUNDY LACE',
'VINCENT VAN GOGH' [↗]

Best for perennial planting
NONE AT BLACKLANDS

Best for cutting
'HAMILTON', 'LAMBADA',
'SWAN WINGS'

Fringed, or fimbriated, tulips look as though they have been attacked with pinking shears, the edges of their petals shredded all the way round. Mutants of Single Earlies, these are not easy to place in a garden context, and I certainly wouldn't want to try to perennialize them. Still, they are fun in a slightly crazy way, so I occasionally use them in container plantings and grow a couple of varieties for cutting. They are surprisingly popular with some of my customers. Fringed tulips were originally grouped with Parrot tulips, and earned their own division only in 1981.

DIVISION 8

VIRIDIFLORA
Late-flowering and long-lasting

Best for containers
'GOLDEN ARTIST', 'GREEN KING'
(SYN. 'EVERGREEN')

Best for perennial planting
'ARTIST', 'CHINA TOWN', 'FLAMING
SPRINGGREEN' |↗|, 'GROENLAND',
'SPRING GREEN', 'VIRICHIC'

Best for cutting
'DOLL'S MINUET', 'ESPERANTO',
'PIMPERNEL'

A Viridiflora tulip is identified by streaks or a wash of green on the outside of its petals. They are often lily-flowered in shape, although some, such as 'Golden Artist', have more rounded petals. They possess excellent perennial properties, one theory being that the presence of green in the petals, in addition to the leaves and stems, allows them to produce more energy through photosynthesis to bulk up the bulb for the next year's flowering. The Viridiflora division was introduced as recently as 1981, but tulips marked with green have been recorded since they were illustrated by Basilius Besler in his *Hortus Eystettensis* of 1613.

REMBRANDT

Late-flowering

Best for containers
ANY, GIVEN THE CORRECT SOIL
AND DRAINAGE

Best for perennial planting
NONE AT BLACKLANDS

Best for cutting
'ABSALON', 'INSULINDE' [↗],
'THE LIZARD', 'SASKIA'

The Rembrandt division is the home of variegated or rectified tulips. The rarefied broken Dutch varieties, immortalized by artists (including Rembrandt, although he was not the most prolific painter of them) in the seventeenth and eighteenth centuries, are placed here, along with the beautiful but less refined broken old Krelage Darwin cultivars. Broken English Florists' tulips with their Rose, Bybloemen and Bizarre colouration and symmetrical markings also belong in this group, as do more modern introductions (such as 'Black and White') bred in the vein of the old broken tulips. Division 9 has become a catch-all for a diversity of broken tulips that have been thrown together regardless of date or origin, on the basis that they are all rectified or variegated and potentially carriers of Tulip Breaking Virus. Some tulips, among them 'Helmar' and 'Striped Sail' (both Division 3), are often incorrectly classed as Rembrandts.

PARROT

Late-flowering

Best for containers
'BLUE PARROT',
'ESTELLA RIJNVELD'

Best for perennial planting
'BLACK PARROT'

Best for cutting
'APRICOT PARROT',
'FLAMING PARROT' ↗

Parrot tulips' petals are lacerated (irregularly cut and split) and twisted, which lends them a freakish, feathery appearance. The division is named for the similarity of the flower bud to a parrot's beak (and the petals to feathers), and perhaps also because of the garish colours often found in such tulips. They have been called Dragon tulips, most famously by the painter and botanist Pierre-Joseph Redouté. They are frequently variegated – which adds to their allure – and sometimes scented. Despite their strikingly contemporary appearance, Parrots have been grown since 1665. They are sports of Single Late and Triumph tulips that come true only from offsets; repeated attempts by commercial breeders to hybridize new seedlings have resulted in tulips with smooth edges. Heavy heads on slender, easily snapped stems make these flowers impractical to grow in the garden. Plant in a sheltered position and expect the odd casualty.

DOUBLE LATE
Late-flowering

Best for containers
'CARNAVAL DE NICE',
'DANCELINE', 'DREAM TOUCH' [•],
'WYNDHAM', 'YELLOW ROSE'

Best for perennial planting
'BLACK HERO'

Best for cutting
'ANGÉLIQUE', 'CHARMING LADY',
'LILAC PERFECTION', 'MOUNT
TACOMA', 'UNCLE TOM'

Longer-stemmed than the Double Earlies and with neater blooms, sometimes multi-headed, the tulips in this division are a mainstay of our garden containers and the flower field. Introduced in Basilius Besler's *Hortus Eystettensis* of 1613, they have remained in fashion ever since (although they certainly have their detractors). The earliest Double Late we grow is 'Yellow Rose', which dates from 1700, and its peony-like flowers radiate antiquity. We plant half a dozen bulbs in a terracotta pot and eagerly anticipate their arrival each year. A new introduction from 2019, 'Wyndham', works well massed in old metal tubs, its strong tones of claret and cream fading gently as the flower matures over several weeks. Like many double tulips, these examples are subtly scented and long-lasting, but sadly – as is the case with double flowers in general – they confound pollinating insects, which cannot find their way to the nectar.

KAUFMANNIANA GROUP

Early-flowering

Best for containers
T. FLORESTA, 'HEART'S DELIGHT',
'ICE STICK' |▪|, 'JOHANN STRAUSS'

Best for perennial planting
T. KAUFMANNIANA

Best for cutting
NONE AT BLACKLANDS

The tulips in this division are also known as Waterlily tulips because of the way the blooms appear both when in bud and when opened out wide to the sun. This division incorporates the wild species tulip *T. kaufmanniana*, and the hybrids and cultivars descended from it or most closely resembling it. Very short, sturdy stems and huge, elongated flowers, generally red, yellow or white with a yellow base. Yellow and white cultivars exhibit red markings around the bases, at the tips or on the reverse of the petals. Glaucous leaves are wide and frequently marked with dark burgundy. Kaufmanniana tulips have strong perennial properties owing to the presence of species blood in them, and they work well in a rock or crevice garden. We grow them in containers for a welcome blast of colour in March.

DIVISION 13

FOSTERIANA GROUP

Early-flowering

Best for containers
'EXOTIC EMPEROR' (SYN. 'WHITE VALLEY'), 'ORANGE EMPEROR'

Best for perennial planting
T. FOSTERIANA, 'PURISSIMA' (SYN. 'WHITE EMPEROR')

Best for cutting
'ALBERT HEIJN', 'FLAMING PURISSIMA' [↗]

Fosteriana tulips (sometimes known as Emperor tulips) are all related to the species *T. fosteriana*, although many also contain genes of *T. kaufmanniana* and *T. greigii*. With large heads and relatively long stems of up to 50 cm (20 in), they are a useful early-flowering tulip for cutting. They also have strong perennial properties, and feature in our naturalized planting schemes at Blacklands. Those in the Purissima series (hybrids between Fosteriana and old Mendel tulips) are among my favourite annual tulips, and of them 'Purissima' (syn. 'White Emperor') and 'Flaming Purissima' are particularly noteworthy. The actual wild, species tulip *T. fosteriana* was integral to the breeding of the old Krelage Darwin hybrids, and is worth growing in its own right for its glossy red flowers and robust, repeat-flowering properties.

DIVISION 14

GREIGII GROUP

Early-flowering

Best for containers
'FÜR ELISE', 'QUEBEC' [↗],
'RED RIDING HOOD', 'SERANO'

Best for perennial planting
T. GREIGII

Best for cutting
NONE AT BLACKLANDS

Tulips in this division are distinctive, with mottled, undulating leaves that grow low to the ground and moderately short stems. The sizeable flowers have an unusual characteristic: the three inner petals like to point straight upwards, while the three outer ones are gently splayed outwards. They most resemble the wild species *T. greigii*, which hails from the Tien Shan mountains and was one of the first Central Asian tulips to be introduced to Europe. *T. greigii* is a rich red (with a great deal of natural variation), and this colour predominates through the division. The short stems mean that these tulips do not lend themselves to cutting. I find they grow best in containers, with a dozen or so of a single variety planted closely together, but I have also seen them work well in a rockery.

MISCELLANEOUS

Early-flowering (most)

Best for containers
'ANNIKA', *T. CRETICA* 'HILDE',
'TINKA'

Best for perennial planting
*T. 'CORNUTA' (SYN. T.
ACUMINATA), T. ORPHANIDEA
WHITTALLII GROUP,
T. SPRENGERI, T. SYLVESTRIS*

Best for cutting
'CYNTHIA', 'PEPPERMINTSTICK' |→|

This division contains all the species tulips that are not in divisions 12, 13 and 14. It includes not only the actual species but also their many, varied cultivated forms – for example, you will find here the species *T. clusiana* (the Lady tulip), which grows wild in the foothills of the Himalayas, plus all its cultivars, including 'Lady Jane', 'Peppermintstick', 'Cynthia', 'Annika' and 'Tinka'. It is difficult to define the characteristics of species tulips, save to say that they are generally smaller in scale and possess a delicacy and purity that are often absent in garden hybrids that have been successively bred and selected for bigger, better flowers. Most of the species tulips and many of their cultivars have strong perennial qualities because of their wild origins, but it can take time and effort to discover which will establish themselves best in your garden. I guarantee they are worth it. Also suited to gravel gardens and rockery plantings. Most come into flower in March, with the exception of *T. aximensis*, which blooms in May, and *T. sprengeri*, which is very late (lasting well into June).

CORONET

Late-flowering

Best for containers
'STRIPED CROWN',
'WHITE LIBERSTAR'

Best for perennial planting
NONE AT BLACKLANDS

Best for cutting
'RED DRESS'

The Coronet division was created in 2018 to accommodate these unusual single-flowering tulips that are reminiscent of a coronet or crown. The flower heads are bulbous at the base and waisted in the middle, while the petals roll inwards at the edges and reflex outwards at the tips. This movement is echoed in the shape of the leaves, which similarly turn in upon themselves and in again towards the stem. All the flower parts, from petals to leaves to stem, are robust and of a denser consistency than those of most tulips. These flowers are not for the faint-hearted, but they have tremendous staying power both in the ground and in the vase. Having said that, I tend not to grow them for cutting, since they lack the movement and delicacy that I am drawn to. They are effective in a mixed container planting, where they provide useful structure.

Top left: *T.* 'Antarctica Flame', 'Disaronno', 'Havran'; Top right: *T.* 'Sanne', 'Wyndham'; Above left: *T.* 'Angélique', 'Antraciet', 'Danceline', 'Dream Touch', 'Nachtwacht', 'Wyndham'; Above right: *T.* 'Black Parrot', 'Menton', 'Queen of Night', 'Slawa'.

This master list of perennial tulips has been built up over many seasons, based upon what we have managed to grow successfully from year to year at Blacklands. We have tried many more cultivars, which failed to thrive, and have come up with this tried-and-tested selection. It should be borne in mind that while these are happy in our soil type, aspects and local climate, they may not be so happy in yours. Experiment with a few bulbs of a variety before committing to a mass planting, and have fun playing with different combinations. I have also included a list of some of my favourite tulip combinations for containers. It has been hard to whittle this down, as we create several different mixes every year – and we change our colour schemes annually too – but these are combinations that I am particularly fond of.

Master Perennial List

T. 'Artist' (Viridiflora)

T. 'Ballerina' (Lily-flowered)

T. 'Black Hero' (Double Late)

T. 'Black Parrot' (Parrot)

T. 'Burgundy' (Lily-flowered)

T. 'Cairo' (Triumph)

T. 'China Pink' (Lily-flowered)

T. 'China Town' (Viridiflora)

T. 'Cornuta' (syn. *T. acuminata*) (Miscellaneous)

T. 'Disaronno' (Triumph)

T. 'Doll's Minuet' (Viridiflora)

T. 'Dom Pedro' (Single Late)

T. 'Flaming Purissima' (Fosteriana)

T. 'Flaming Springgreen' (Viridiflora)

T. 'Gavota' (Triumph)

T. 'Golden Artist' (Viridiflora)

T. 'Greenstar' (Lily-flowered)

T. 'Groenland' (Viridiflora)

T. 'Havran' (Triumph)

T. 'Ivory Floradale' (Darwin Hybrid)

T. 'Jimmy' (Triumph)

T. 'Light and Dreamy' (Darwin Hybrid)

T. 'Marilyn' (Lily-flowered)

T. 'Maytime' (Lily-flowered)

T. 'Menton' (Single Late)

T. 'Mistress Mystic' (Triumph)

T. 'Mystic van Eijk' (Darwin Hybrid)

T. 'Purissima' (syn. 'White Emperor') (Fosteriana)

T. 'Queen of Night' (Single Late)

T. 'Request' (Triumph)

T. 'Ronaldo' (Triumph)

T. 'Shirley' (Triumph)

T. 'Spring Green' (Viridiflora)

T. 'Très Chic' (Lily-flowered)

T. 'Virichic' (Viridiflora)

T. 'White Triumphator' (Lily-flowered)

Favourite Combinations for Container Plantings

T. 'Angélique', 'Antraciet', 'Danceline', 'Dream Touch', 'Nachtwacht', 'Wyndham' (see opposite, bottom left)

T. 'Antarctica Flame', 'Disaronno', 'Havran' (see opposite, top left)

T. 'Apeldoorn's Elite', 'Fly Away', 'Formosa' (see p.243, bottom left)

T. 'Apricot Foxx', 'Black Hero', 'Bleu Aimable', 'Spring Green' (see p.242, bottom right)

T. 'Apricot Foxx', 'Brown Sugar', 'Café Noir' (see pp.180–1)

T. 'Ballade', 'Burgundy', 'China Town', 'Gabriella', 'Sapporo' (see p.243, top right)

T. 'Ballerina', 'Black Bean', 'Black Parrot', 'Slawa' (see p.243, bottom right))

T. 'Belle Époque', 'Black Bean', 'Bleu Aimable', 'Insulinde', 'Jan Reus'

T. 'Black Bean', 'Gabriella', 'Malaika' (syn. 'Brune Wimpel'), 'Sanne', 'Très Chic' (see p.242, top right)

T. 'Black Parrot', 'Estella Rijnveld', 'Jan Reus'

T. 'Black Parrot', 'Menton', 'Queen of Night', 'Slawa' (see opposite, bottom right)

T. 'Café Noir', 'Flaming Springgreen', 'Jimmy', 'Twilight Princess'

T. 'Charming Lady', 'Foxy Foxtrot', 'Orange Princess', 'Wyndham' (see p.184)

T. 'Copper Image', 'Dream Touch', 'Orange Princess' (see p.29)

T. 'Copper Image', 'Foxy Foxtrot', 'Montreaux', 'Uncle Tom', 'Wyndham' (see p.242, top left)

T. 'Dreamer', 'Fantasy Lady', 'Foxy Foxtrot', 'Montreal'

T. 'Dom Pedro', 'Flaming Parrot', 'Françoise', 'Jan Reus', 'Paul Scherer', 'Wallflower' (see p.185)

T. 'Dom Pedro', 'Jan Reus', 'Lilac Love', 'Madras', 'Mistress Mystic', 'Queen of Night' (see p.189)

T. 'Estella Rijnveld', 'Flaming Springgreen', 'Maureen', 'Renegade' (see p.243, top left)

T. 'Sanne', 'Wyndham' (see opposite, top right)

Top left: *T.* 'Copper Image', 'Foxy Foxtrot', 'Montreaux', 'Uncle Tom', 'Wyndham'; Top right: *T.* 'Black Bean', 'Gabriella', 'Malaika' (syn. 'Bruine Wimpel'), 'Sanne', 'Très Chic'; Above left: *T.* 'Antarctica Flame', 'Green King', 'Sapporo' and 'Spring Green'; Above right: *T.* 'Apricot Foxx', 'Black Hero', 'Bleu Aimable', 'Spring Green'.

Top left: *T*. 'Estella Rijnveld', 'Flaming Springgreen', 'Maureen', 'Renegade'; Top right: *T*. 'Ballade', 'Burgundy' (not shown in flower), 'China Town', 'Gabriella', 'Sapporo'; Above left: *T*. 'Apeldoorn's Elite', 'Fly Away', 'Formosa'; Above right: *T*. 'Ballerina', 'Black Bean', 'Black Parrot', 'Slawa'.

Our Environmental Ethos

Our whole property at Blacklands is organically certified by the Soil Association UK, and the flower field, garden, pasture, woodland, riverbanks and livestock are all managed and maintained to their stringent standards. We try to purchase our tulip bulbs from organic sources. When that is not practical, special dispensation (called derogation) is required and the tulips cannot be marketed as organic for their first growing season. We are subject to yearly Soil Association inspections during the course of which all our paperwork is studied, our store cupboards are opened and growing areas visited. Even the feed for our six bantam chickens is scrutinized.

We do not use any pesticides, herbicides or chemically synthesized fertilizers. Seaweed is our favourite feed for tulips, but most important of all is feeding the soil itself and working with nature's systems and cycles. Implementing natural methods, including crop rotation, green manures, biological pest control and companion planting, is normal, everyday practice for us. We have drilled a borehole and fitted it with a series of (endlessly troublesome) pumps to supply the walled garden with water, and we are also permitted to extract a quota from the River Marden. Black British bees live in hives at the far reaches of the garden, and I like to think that we provide them with a plethora of flowers to feed on, which they kindly pollinate for us in return.

Craftsmanship is central to our ethos, perhaps best evidenced in the range of plant supports constructed from home-grown coppiced hazel that are a feature of the garden. The shelters that protect our most prized tulips from the elements are things of beauty that serve a useful purpose, as are the hazel domes in the rose garden.

Wherever possible we try to reduce our input, recycle materials and reuse tulip bulbs.

Looking After our Soil

We are blessed with beautiful, rich, black soil at Blacklands, but growing successive crops of tulips for cutting, or growing historic tulips year after year, can take its toll and reduce the fertility of soil and the biological activity within it. In high summer, after the tulip season is well and truly over and the historics have been lifted, we mulch the beds with a thick layer of our home-made compost, which includes garden and household waste, the contents of the chicken coop and well-rotted manure from our stable of horses. Over the years we have experimented by adding different ingredients to the compost bays, such as charcoal and other inoculants; we are open to new ideas and like to try out different organic products and methods.

When the beds aren't full of tulips – either during the summer months after they have been lifted or because they are tulip-free for three years out of four in line with our rotation scheme – some are planted with dahlias or annual flower crops, others are filled with green manure and a certain number are used for vegetables for the house, such as squash or potatoes. The aim is for the soil to remain covered by living plants so that it can maintain its structure, stay teeming with microbial action and sequester carbon.

The woodland beds that house *Tulipa sylvestris* are mulched with leaf manure collected from around the property in late autumn and stored in a large bay, while beds that are home to permanent planting schemes in the walled garden and rose garden are mulched with compost or an organic soil improver. Perennial tulips planted in grass are considered responsible adults and left to look after themselves.

Growing Mediums

We have a mixture of ground-level and raised beds in the flower field. The ground-level beds have been cut straight out of the earth with the aid of a turf-cutter and receive no additions for the first year of growing (apart from sand to improve drainage, if necessary), but thereafter we add a thick mulch to the surface once a year. For the raised beds we make a mix consisting of one third loam, one third compost (either our recipe or bought in) and one third horticultural sand.

All tulips in containers, whether species, historic or garden varieties, are planted in a mix consisting of equal parts of our own loam, peat-free potting compost and sand. If you don't have direct access to free-draining loam, it is perfectly acceptable to leave it out, and instead make a mixture of two thirds potting compost and one third sand. There have been times when we have left the sand out for the annual tulips in containers, but we always include it for species tulips, which require excellent drainage.

Planting, Irrigation and Feeding

I start planting the annual tulips in late October, move on to species and historics in November, and finish some time in December (usually just before Christmas). Occasionally the quiet days between Christmas and New Year are spent packing bulbs into pots in a frantic attempt to get them all done. I tend to plant English Florists' tulips last of all, for that brings about a later flowering period, thereby increasing my chances of having a decent range of flowers to take to the Tulip Society's Annual Show in mid-May. Planting late also gives the benefit of soil cleansed from pathogens by the first frosts. For detailed information on growing the different types of tulip (species, Dutch Historic tulips, English Florists' tulips, annual tulips), see the relevant chapters.

Whether or not to water tulips immediately after planting depends on the weather. In a prolonged warm, dry spell it is a good idea, but if temperatures are set to drop below freezing or rain is on the horizon, it doesn't make much sense.

Rarely do we water over the winter, but it is becoming necessary to do so in March, April and May, and containers will certainly need irrigating during the spring months. Always check the soil for moisture beneath the surface with your finger, as it can appear quite dry on top but actually be perfectly moist an inch or two below. Adding a thin layer of gravel to the surface in smaller containers helps to conserve moisture in the soil.

Any watering at Blacklands is carried out by hand with a hose or watering can. We installed an automated irrigation system in the flower field a few years ago, but it was more trouble than it was worth, becoming torn and blocked in the first season. It is straightforward to water large beds with a hose, and smaller

beds with a watering can. Not only can the quantity be varied according to the weather, but this hands-on approach also affords the opportunity to check all the tulips at close quarters.

The borehole sited just outside the walled garden feeds a large stone trough (see opposite), and the ritual of dipping a watering can repeatedly in and out as it is replenished is both satisfying and meditative. Rainwater is purer than mains water, without trace elements of chemicals and chlorine. Water butts for collecting it are affordable and easy to install; make sure they are positioned to catch as much roof run-off as possible, and keep them covered for child safety. Our greenhouse has an old tank installed at one end that is fed by rainwater directed from the roof guttering. It is important to note that any tulips left in the ground over the summer should be allowed to dry out and have a period of dormancy. During these months, take care to avoid sprinkling herbaceous beds where there are tulip plantings.

Tulips planted in the field and in containers are fed with a dilute organic seaweed feed once they are actively in growth, usually once every two weeks. After flowering we administer one final feed to the historic tulips before they are left to die back. Feed can stain flowers and foliage, so we use a watering can without a rose so that the flow from the spout can be directed at the base of the plants rather than overhead. Small-scale tulip growers are divided between those who feed with seaweed and those who choose a tomato feed rich in potassium. The former works well for us.

Deadheading

Spent flower heads should be snapped off right at the top, leaving the stem and leaves intact to photosynthesize and provide energy for the formation of new bulbs. I deadhead by hand, grasping the very top of the stem between my first two fingers and thumb; it is handy to have a trug alongside for the heads, which are thrown on to the compost heap.

Species tulips benefit from being deadheaded whether they are in containers or planted in the open garden, to help them direct their energy into the production of new bulbs for the next flowering season. This obviously isn't practical with large naturalized plantings, but it is straightforward for smaller areas and containers. The exception to the deadheading rule is *T. sprengeri*, a species tulip that spreads efficiently by seed (see p.64).

Historic varieties, both Dutch and English Florists' tulips, should always be deadheaded straight after flowering has finished, to prevent the formation of seed heads and the build-up of decaying petals in the beds, which increases the risk of disease. Annual tulips in perennial plantings benefit from deadheading, but in the rougher areas around the compost bays I leave them be.

Pests and Diseases

Deer love tulips, and the only way to keep them out is with a tall fence or by grazing sheep nearby (deer hate sheep even more than they love tulips). Squirrels will do anything for a bulb or two, but can be thwarted by chicken-wire hats, sharp sprigs of holly plunged into the soil or, for herbaceous plantings, chilli powder or flakes. Once the bulbs are properly anchored by their roots (usually when the shoots are about 8 cm/3 in tall) they are much harder to steal. Rabbits can be kept out with fencing, which must extend down into the soil to stop them from digging underneath. For mice, we lay traps loaded with chunks of chocolate, and for rats we speed-dial the pest controller. Slugs are kept largely at bay using nematodes and organically-approved slug pellets (top-dressing containers with gravel helps, too). Moles and voles are an issue for which I have not found a good solution, although trials of battery-operated sonars seem promising.

Watch out for other people's dogs in the garden during the tulip flowering period, as they can trample a display, and watch out for the reaction of family members in particular when you tell them their pets are not welcome. Holding a National Collection of tulips is an excellent excuse to ban them (the dogs, that is – family members are always welcome).

Disease is most easily prevented by growing tulips outside, rather than under cover. It helps to plant the bulbs slightly further apart than normal, so that air can circulate and it is easier to extract any plant that shows signs of disease. We quarantine all new historic bulbs, and have a 'sick bay' where we plant any bulbs that looked remotely suspicious during the previous season.

I live in fear of tulip fire, because it could wipe out my historic collection, but thankfully it is quite rare. It may be possible to halt early progress by tearing off affected leaves, but it is usually advisable to dig up entire specimens. Keep a close eye on neighbouring plants for signs of contagion. We burn any plants on the bonfire if we are worried, and always disinfect the tools we have used. The RHS offers laboratory analysis to members, which can provide much-needed reassurance, since there are other types of botrytis that are not to be feared in the same way. When harvesting historic bulbs, it is good practice to peel a few to check there are no telltale black spots hiding under the tunic.

Stem and bulb nematode (eelworm) is new to me, and I am now on the lookout for stunted, distorted growth in my tulips. Beds that have shown signs of it must be left fallow for three years, as any plant can play host and prolong an infection.

Tulip Breaking Virus (TBV) is spread by aphids and is permanently present in broken tulips. It is a threat to our breeder tulips, and I try to mitigate this with careful husbandry (keeping broken varieties at a distance from breeders and handling the two types separately). Ladybirds will reduce the number of aphids, another benefit of organic gardening without insecticides. TBV is regarded as a risk by the commercial tulip industry, which also has to contend with Tulip Virus X (TVX) and the fungus fusarium (*Fusarium oxysporum* f. sp. *tulipae*), among other diseases. Thankfully Blacklands has not yet been affected by these.

Cutting and Conditioning the Flowers

I tend to pull annual tulips to sell, rather than cutting them, because extracting them with the bulb intact affords extra stem length and avoids the laborious task of digging up bulbs at the end of the season – everyone's least favourite job. Sometimes the bulbs won't come out of the soil easily, in which case I cut the stems with a pair of secateurs as close to the ground as possible.

The flowers are loaded on to a trolley (in buckets of water if cut, or piled flat when on the bulb) and taken straight to my workshop in the coach house, where the bulbs are excised, the bottom leaves stripped and stems quickly rinsed of soil. The flowers are placed in clean buckets of water and left for a few hours (or overnight) in the cool of the coach house, where the walls are thick and the temperature constant. This is called conditioning. I do not wrap them in paper to keep them upright, or use the old trick of piercing the top of the stems with a pin to prevent them from moving, nor do I feed them with any solutions. I want them to be as natural as possible, and that includes allowing them to twist and turn. Within twenty-four hours they are on their way to their final destination, as fresh as can be.

Lifting and Storing the Bulbs

Annual tulips in containers are lifted in May and left to dry in well-ventilated trays under cover in the yard. A single layer of bulbs allows better air circulation and prevents mould. The dead plant matter is removed over the summer, leaving the bulbs ready to plant in late autumn.

Historic varieties grown in the field and in pots are left in situ until early July (or June if the weather has been hot and sunny), and excavated carefully before being stored in labelled racks. The soil is removed from each bulb to check for signs of disease or damage, and any remaining stem or leaf is removed by hand; as part of the process I scratch over the basal plate with my fingernail, as this area is most likely to harbour disease. I also peel the tunics from a few of each variety, to check for signs of tulip fire.

Do not worry if bulblets become detached from the main bulb, but do keep them safe and labelled; I store them with the larger bulbs. Any bulblet smaller than about 1.5 cm (½ in) will take a couple of years to flower, so if you already have a decent quantity of a cultivar you might want to limit what you keep or you will soon run out of space (and time).

Storage racks should be under cover, but with adequate airflow and protection from vermin; we cover the structures with heavy-duty mesh and set traps. Check the storage areas regularly – in 2022 we discovered a rat's nest in some 'Insulinde' bulbs.

We don't like to grow tulips under cover, but this selection of Dutch
Historic tulips was planted in the polytunnel by rats, rather than me –
they raided the storage boxes one autumn and this row of beautiful
flowers appeared from the rat run the following April.

Jobs for Autumn

• Sort new bulbs as they come in, looking out for any orders that have been incorrectly supplied. Store bulbs in a cool, dry place until you are ready to plant them.
• Prepare the tulip beds. Dig out the soil shortly before planting time, heaping it on groundsheets.
• Buy horticultural sand, making sure it is clean and free-draining. This will be used in tulip beds, for the base of planting holes when naturalizing tulips in the garden and in the soil mix for container tulips.
• Buy peat-free multipurpose compost for preparing soil mixes.
• Buy gravel for top-dressing smaller containers.
• Prepare containers, making sure that they are clean, drilling drainage holes in the bottom as necessary and gathering a good supply of crocks.
• Sort labels and marker pens (you can never have enough pens). We use slate labels in the walled garden and large plastic ones in the flower field, removing the previous year's writing with nail-polish remover so that we can reuse as many labels as possible.
• Buy rolls of chicken wire to protect containers from squirrel raids and industrial-sized bags of chilli powder or flakes to deter them from herbaceous plantings.
• Bulb planting starts at the end of October and continues to the end of December. Look at the weather forecast to avoid freezing or rainy days.
• Weed fallow tulip beds and plant with green manure. We use an organic over-winter mix that can be planted between mid-September and mid-October.

Jobs for Winter

• Bulb planting continues right up to Christmas. English Florists' tulips will benefit from later planting, as it leads to a later flowering time to coincide with the Annual Show in mid-May.
• Ensure that all containers, large and small, are protected with chicken-wire hats immediately upon planting, and scatter chilli wherever species or annual tulips are planted in beds.
• Monitor fences to make sure they are deer-proof, and keep an eye out for moles and voles.
• Check supplies of protective netting ready for the spring, to act as windbreaks between broken and breeder tulips (to help prevent the transmission of TBV by aphids). Erect hazel frames, ready to be covered with netting.

Jobs for Spring

• Make sure all labels are clearly visible and legible.
• Weed the tulip beds when the temperatures start to rise and the first weeds appear, for they will compete with the tulips for light and water. This also makes life much easier later in the season when tulips have to be lifted and stored.
• Water during prolonged dry periods, checking down into the soil for moisture levels rather than relying on surface observations. Irrigation is becoming increasingly necessary during the long, hot springs brought about by climate change. Containers are particularly vulnerable to both waterlogging and drying out, so check them frequently.
• Feed tulips for cutting and in containers with a dilute organic seaweed feed every two weeks, and once more after they have finished flowering.
• Take plenty of notes and photographs for your records, and jot down which tulips you do and don't like, as an aide-memoire for the following year's orders.
• Check daily for signs of disease, carefully tearing off spotted or mildewed foliage and removing any tulip that looks suspicious.
• Pull or cut annual tulips for use as cut flowers.
• Deadhead historic and perennially grown tulips (including species tulips) as soon as they go over, so that the energy goes back into creating a new bulb and offsets.
• Empty container plantings soon after flowering, to free them up for summer displays. Species tulips can be left under cover in their pots and repotted in fresh soil mix later in the year.

Jobs for Summer

• Lift historic bulbs once the foliage has died back, but before it has disappeared completely; a bulb will be much harder to locate once it is no longer marked by its stem.
• Store historic tulips in racks under cover, making sure they are carefully labelled. Likewise container grown bulbs that will be recycled in perennial plantings.
• Weed the tulip beds. There's nothing like a freshly weeded bed to cheer you up, and it makes it much easier to harvest the bulbs you want to keep. Mulch beds as necessary.
• Plant annual flowers or green manure in the newly vacated tulip beds.
• Update rotation plans so that any bed used for cropping or for historics is tulip-free for three years. This is particularly important for historic tulips, since a whole collection could be wiped out by tulip fire lurking in the soil.
• Disinfect containers so they are ready to be planted later in the year. Scrub large containers with a dilute natural disinfectant and dip small ones into a barrel of the same solution.
• Order new bulbs to be delivered in the autumn. Don't go mad with the ordering – all the tulips have to have homes, and planting takes considerable time and effort. We have all been defeated by a final bag or two of gently mouldering tulip bulbs discovered some time after the New Year. On the other hand, you can never have enough tulips.

Anther The part of the flower at the top of the **stamen** that produces and contains pollen.

Anthocyanin The pigment in the outer layers of a **petal** that 'breaks' in a **broken tulip**, revealing the **base** colour in a myriad of patterns.

'Art Shades' A range of Dutch breeder tulips in moody, indefinable yellows, browns and oranges that were the height of fashion at the beginning of the twentieth century, particularly in the United States. Examples of this type of tulip are 'Dom Pedro' (1911), 'Dillenburg' (1916) and 'Old Times' (1919).

Base Also known as ground, base colour, base plate, basal blotch, basal splodge or basal patch. The central part of the inside of the tulip, at the base of the **petals**, which is generally white, yellow or black (sometimes khaki or blue). The base is one of the most prized parts of an **English Florists' tulip**, and must be clearly defined and of a clean yellow or white.

Bizarre A tulip that has a yellow base with brown to red **petals**. The term is now rarely applied to **Dutch Historic tulips**, but is one of the three accepted colourways for an **English Florists' tulip** (*see also* Bybloemen, Rose). Also referred to in old records as 'Bizarren'.

Breeder tulip Also known as mother tulip or self. A plain-coloured tulip not (visibly) affected by **Tulip Breaking Virus** that is used as breeding stock to produce **broken tulips** (affected by TBV) or solid, plain-coloured progeny. Breeder tulips are prized and protected in their own right in the case of **Dutch Historic** and **English Florists' tulips**.

Broken tulip Also known as a rectified, variegated, striped or Rembrandt tulip. A patterned tulip that has been infected by **Tulip Breaking Virus** and has 'broken' (from a plain-coloured **breeder**) into **flames** and **feathers**. Such tulips have been prized since the sixteenth century, when they exchanged hands for fortunes and gave rise to the period known as **Tulipmania**, and they are still revered today. Broken tulips are outlawed in the bulb industry because they pose a risk of contamination to commercial crops.

Bulblet *see* Offset

Bybloemen A tulip that has a white base with lilac to purple **petals** (*see also* Bizarre, Rose). Also referred to in old records as 'Violetten'. *See also* English Florists' tulip.

Corona Also known as halo. A band of colour surrounding the **base** of a tulip. Often a lighter shade of the base colour, but sometimes a contrasting shade, such as indigo-blue or a sludgy green.

Cottage tulips An old group of tulips dating back to the mid-eighteenth century, now incorporated into the Single Late **division** (Division 5). Late-flowering.

Crocks Pieces of old terracotta pots used to cover drainage hole(s) at the bottom of a container, to prevent the soil from being washed out when watered or in the rain.

Cultivar A genetically distinct individual clone that has been **selected** for propagation from a wild plant or deliberately bred. A cultivar name follows the genus name and is given initial capitals and quotation marks: for example, *Tulipa* 'Dom Pedro'.

Division There are currently sixteen different tulip divisions, from Single Early (Division 1) to Coronet (Division 16). Each one has a name and a number (see p.223).

Dropper A small new bulb descending on a shoot from the main, **mother** bulb.

Duc van Tol tulip A race of diminutive, jewel-coloured tulips dating back more than 400 years.

Dutch Historic tulip The term I use for rare, unusual tulips that are generally not available commercially.

Eelworm *see* Stem and bulb nematode

English Florists' tulip Tulips bred in England from the beginning of the nineteenth century, and exhibited at tulip shows by 'florists' (specialist flower growers). Their hallmarks include a shallow, hemispherical cup shape, three different colourways (**Rose**, **Bybloemen** and **Bizarre**), and distinctive **flamed** and **feathered** markings.

Feathered A term generally used of **English Florists' tulips** to denote a concentration of fine markings on the **petal** edges of a **broken** flower, and one of the two broken forms of English Florists' tulip that has been infected by **Tulip Breaking Virus** (*see also* Flamed). Less heavily patterned than a flamed tulip, a feathered example should ideally have no beam of colour running up the centre of the petals.

Filament A slender stalk that supports the **anther** at the centre of a flower. Together the filament and anther make up the **stamen**. Tulips exhibited on the showbench must have six filaments and anthers (as I found out to my cost when I accidentally exhibited one with five).

Flamed An intensification of the top layer of colour up the central beam of the **petal**, branching out and connecting with **feathering** around the edges. One of the two **broken** forms of an **English Florists' tulip** that has been infected by **Tulip Breaking Virus** (*see also* Feathered).

Glaucous (of leaves) Having a blue tinge.

Green manure A fast-growing crop used to cover bare soil, to build and maintain soil fertility and structure. My favourite green manures for empty tulip beds are purple tansy (*Phacelia tanacetifolia*) and brown or Indian mustard (*Brassica juncea*).

Halo see **Corona**

Hooking (of **petals**) Curving slightly inwards at the tips.

Hybrid The product of cross-fertilization between two different species or varieties. Confusingly, the terms 'hybrid'

and 'cultivar' are frequently used interchangeably in bulb catalogues and other literature relating to tulips.

Jaspis An old (and now rarely used) term describing the spotted markings of a **broken** tulip, alluding to the markings of the stone jaspis or jasper.

Lanceolate (of a leaf) Lance- or sword-shaped, wider at the base than at the midpoint, and tapering to a point.

Mendel tulip An old race of tulips bred in the early to mid-twentieth century, from crosses between **Duc van Tol** and Krelage Darwin varieties. Now incorporated into the Triumph **division** (Division 3).

Microendemic Specific to a very restricted area.

Midrib A vein up the centre of a **petal**. Often prominent and, in a tulip, frequently flushed with another colour or tone.

Mother A mature bulb of a good size that produces **offsets** each year. *See also* Breeder tulip.

Neo-tulipa A tulip that has made the reverse journey from garden cultivation to native plant and, because of its captive origin, is usually easier than many to naturalize in a garden setting.

Offset Also known as bulblet or daughter bulb. A small bulb growing from the base of a **mother** bulb and genetically identical to it. Offsets can be carefully separated and used to propagate more tulips, although they usually take two or three years to flower, depending on size. Propagation by offsets gives rise to offspring that are true (identical) to the mother, whereas propagation by seed does not.

Pedicel A slender stem that attaches an individual flower to an inflorescence (cluster of flowers).

Peony-flowered A tulip with a large, double head formed of ruffled **petals**, giving the appearance of a peony (*Paeonia* spp.). Peony-flowered tulips are

categorized as Double Early (**Division** 2) or Double Late (**Division** 11).

Petal A part of the flower enclosed by the **sepal**. In tulips (and lilies) petals and sepals are indistinguishable, and are referred to as **tepals**, but I refer to them as 'petals' throughout this book since that term is more commonly recognized.

Potyvirus The largest genus of plant viruses, spread by aphids. **Tulip Breaking Virus** is a potyvirus.

Quartering Gaps between the **petals** at their bases, most noticeable when the petal is fully open. This is an undesirable trait in an **English Florists' tulip**, where the petals should overlap slightly.

Raised (of a new tulip) Bred from seed after the successful cross-pollination of two **cultivars**. The person who achieves this is recognized as the 'raiser'.

Rectified *see* Broken

Recurved (of **petals**) Curving backwards, also known as 'reflexed'.

Rembrandt *see* Broken Tulip

Rose A tulip with a white base and pink to red **petals**. Also referred to as 'Rosen' or 'Rozen' in old records. *See also* Bizarre, Bybloemen, English Florists' tulip.

Rotation The systematic movement of a crop from one area to another in successive years, to prevent pathogens that might be in the soil from infecting subsequent plantings. Usually practised on a four-year cycle. At Blacklands we rotate our tulips through a series of beds in the flower field. After tulips have been grown in a bed, we use it for other crops, such as annual flowers, or sow **green manure** for the next three years.

Selection The practice of retaining plants with the most desirable traits and discarding others.

Self-coloured Also known as a self. Either a plain-coloured tulip (as in a **breeder**) with a contrasting **base** colour, or a single coloured tulip with no contrasting base, for instance 'Duc van Tol Primrose'.

Sepal A part of the flower that encloses the **petal**. In tulips (and lilies) sepals and petals are indistinguishable, and are referred to as **tepals**.

Species tulip Also known as botanical tulip. An original, wild tulip that has not been hybridized (bred), and its subspecies, varieties or forms.

Sport A mutant tulip that bears no obvious resemblance to its parent. Many new tulips start life in this way.

Stamen The male reproductive part of a flower, consisting of **filament** and **anther**.

Stem and bulb nematode Also known as eelworm. A pathogen (*Ditylenchus dipsaci*) that can cause stunted, distorted growth in tulips, as well as other flower bulbs and vegetables, among them onions and garlic.

Stigma The top segment of the female part of a flower, visible as a prominent, sticky protuberance that is receptive to pollen.

Stolon A horizonal shoot that gives rise to a new plant. Many **species tulips** spread by means of stolons, and are therefore said to be stoloniferous. Stolons are usually above ground, but in tulips they are underground.

Tepal The **sepal** or **petal** of a tulip (or lily), so-called because in these flowers the sepals and petals are indistinguishable. However, throughout this book I use the term 'petal'.

Top-dress To cover the soil surface with a layer of grit or horticultural sand, for a smart appearance, to prevent splashback onto the sides of the pot and to retain moisture in the soil by limiting evaporation.

Tulip Breaking Virus (TBV) Also known as tulip mosaic virus. A **potyvirus** particular to tulips that causes a plain tulip to 'break' into a **broken**, patterned one. It was first

identified by Dorothy Cayley in 1927 at the John Innes Institute in London. Until then the cause of the **flaming** and **feathering** that had given rise to **Tulipmania** was a mystery and the subject of endless conjecture. Several different strains of TBV are known.

Tulip fire A fungus (*Botrytis tulipae*) that strikes fear into the hearts of growers every tulip season. Particularly prevalent during warm, wet springs, it can destroy entire plantings and will overwinter in soil and bulbs. The telltale signs are spotted, mouldy flowers and leaves. Infected bulbs will have visible black scales on the surface and should be burned at the time of lifting (they must never enter the composting system). Commercial crops and collections are regularly sprayed with fungicide to prevent occurrences of tulip fire, whereas under my organic system I have to depend solely on ultra-careful husbandry. We **rotate** all our tulips in a four-year cycle to help prevent the spread of tulip fire.

Tulipmania Also known as Tulipomania. The period between 1634 and 1637 when the Dutch nation became gripped by a fever for tulips. It is considered the first economic bubble, when tulip prices in the Netherlands were ludicrously inflated and speculators made their fortunes buying and selling bulbs – then lost those fortunes just as quickly when the bottom fell out of the market.

Tunic The thin brown outer coat of a tulip bulb. Botanists can identify one **species tulip** from another in their wild, native habitats from minute differences between their tunics.

Undulate (of a leaf) Wavy-edged.

Vernalization A prolonged period of cold that tulip bulbs require for flowering to be stimulated. In warm climates or in large-scale, year-round production, this cold period is brought about artificially.

Viridiflora Tulips that have an element of green in their flowers, caused by

extra chlorophyll. The presence of this additional chlorophyll is thought to make Viridiflora tulips more reliably perennial, since they produce extra energy through photosynthesis for the formation of the following year's bulb. There is a **division** (Division 8) devoted to Viridiflora tulips.

RESOURCES

Bulb Suppliers

UK
Bloms Bulbs
Broadleigh Gardens
De Jager
Farmer Gracy
Jacques Amand International
Kevock Garden Plants
Organic Bulbs
Peter Nyssen
Pottertons Nursery
Sarah Raven

Netherlands
De Warande (Sterkebollen)
Ecobulbs (organic)
Floratuin
Fluwel
Huiberts Organic Flower Bulbs
Natural Bulbs (organic)
Nijssen Tuin

Germany
Kiepenkerl
Gärtner Pötschke

USA
Brent & Becky's
Colorblends
John Scheepers, Beauty from Bulbs
Longfield Gardens
Old House Gardens (Heirloom Bulbs)
RoozenGaarde
Van Engelen Inc.
White Flower Farm

General Suppliers (UK)
Apsley Farms (composts
 and mulches)
Cotswold Seeds (green manures)
Dalefoot Composts (composts
 and mulches)
Dragonfli (biological pest control)
Flowers from the Farm (directory
 of British cut-flower suppliers)
The Land Gardeners (compost)
Melcourt Industries (composts
 and mulches)

Places to Visit

UK
Cambridge University Botanic Garden
 (Plant Heritage National Collection of
 Tulipa spp. and Primary Hybrids)
Constable Burton Estate, North Yorkshire
Forde Abbey, Somerset
Hever Castle & Gardens, Kent
Morton Hall Gardens, Worcestershire
Pashley Manor Gardens, East Sussex
RHS Garden Wisley, Surrey
Royal Botanic Gardens Kew, London (Plant
 Heritage National Collection of *Tulipa* spp.)

The Netherlands
Hortus Bulborum, Limmen
Keukenhof, Lisse
Poldertuin Anna Paulowna ('Klein
 Keukenhof'), Anna Paulowna

Rest of World
Canadian Tulip Festival, Ottowa
Emirgan Park Tulip Festival, Emirgan Tulip
 Gardens, Istanbul
Patthana Garden, County Wicklow,
 Republic of Ireland
Skagit Valley Tulip Festival, Mount
 Vernon, WA, USA
Tonami Tulip Park, Toyama, Japan

Further Reading

Atasoy, Nurhan. *A Garden for the Sultan:
 Gardens and Flowers in the Ottoman
 Culture*. Kitap Yayinevi, 2011.
Blunt, Wilfred. *Tulips and Tulipomania*.
 Basilisk Press, 1977.
Daffodil, Snowdrop and Tulip Yearbook.
 RHS, annually.
Duthie, Ruth. *Florists' Flowers and
 Societies*. Shire Publications, 1988.
Dykes, W. R. *Notes on Tulip Species*.
 Herbert Jenkins, 1930.
Everett, Diana. *The Genus Tulipa: Tulips
 of the World*. Royal Botanic Gardens,
 Kew, 2013.
Fisher, Celia. *Tulip*. Reaktion Books, 2017.
Flames and Feathers: English Florists' Tulips.
 Wakefield & North of England Tulip
 Society, 2012. (First published as *English
 Florists' Tulips: Into the Twenty first
 Century*.)
Hall, A. Daniel. *The Book of the Tulip*.
 Martin Hopkinson, 1929.
— *The Genus Tulipa*. RHS, 1940.
Jacob, Joseph. *Hardy Bulbs for Amateurs*.
 Country Life, 1924.
Leijenhorst, Leslie. *Hortus Bulborum:
 Schatkamer van historische
 bolgewassen/Treasury of Historical
 Bulbs*. Wormeveer, 2004.
Maddock, James. *The Florists' Directory;
 or a Treatise on the Culture of Flowers*
 [1792]. Forgotten Books, 2018.
Old Flames: English Florists' Tulips. Yorkshire
 Sculpture Park and WNETS, 2006.
Pavord, Anna. *The Tulip*. New edn.
 Bloomsbury, 2019. (First edn, 1999.)
RHS. *Plant Finder 2023*. RHS, 2023.
RHS. *Report of the Tulip Nomenclature
 Committee, 1914–1915*. Spottiswoode,
 Ballantyne & Co., 1917.
Segal, Sam, and Klara Alen, trans. Judith
 Deitch. *Dutch and Flemish Flower
 Pieces: Paintings, Drawings and Prints
 up to the Nineteenth Century*. Brill, 2020.
Slater, John. *A Descriptive Catalogue of
 Tulips, Together with Its History, Mode of
 Cultivation, &c.* Orr & Co., 1843.
Smith, Matthew, and Grete Smith. *A
 Gardener's Guide to Tulips: Ensuring
 Successful Cultivation in the Garden*.
 Crowood Press, 2023.
Van Scheepen, J., ed.. *Classified List and
 International Register of Tulip Names*.
 KAVB, 1996 (also 2005 supplement).
Wilford, Richard. *Tulips: Species and Hybrids
 for the Gardener*. Timber Press, 2006.
— *The Plant Lover's Guide to Tulips*.
 Timber Press, 2015.

Useful Websites

Dutch Royal General Bulbgrowers'
 Association (KAVB): www.kavb.nl
Hortus Tulipus: www.oldtulips.org
National Gardening Association (USA):
 www.garden.org
National Garden Scheme (UK):
 www.ngs.org.uk
Plant Heritage: www.plantheritage.org.uk
Royal Horticultural Society: www.rhs.org.uk
Soil Association: www.soilassociation.org
Wakefield & North of England Tulip
 Society: www.tulipsociety.co.uk

AUTHOR'S ACKNOWLEDGEMENTS

This book is dedicated to Ed,
with endless love and gratitude.

Victoria Clarke has been a phenomenal commissioning editor and editor, with an enviably sharp memory. It has been a pleasure to work with her. Rosanna Fairhead copy-edited my text with a light touch and a good sense of humour, and Clare Churly proofread the final version in layout. The book's designer, Paco Lacasta, has created a design with which I am delighted, while putting up with my many comments and requests along the way. Lily Rodgers oversaw production and helped the tulips to shine brightly on the pages. Together you have done my tulips proud.

The photographer Andrew Montgomery captured the tulips and garden perfectly with his inimitable eye over three long seasons, demonstrating commendable patience while the tulips (and I) woke up in the morning. I don't blame you, Andrew, if you never want to see a tulip again.

Britt Willoughby Dyer started recording my tulip collection more than ten years ago, and her pictures never fail to encapsulate their essence. I am delighted that they are featured in this book.

The Committee of the Wakefield and North of England Tulip Society kindly read and fact-checked Chapter 3 on English Florists' tulips, and donated a selection of prize-winning tulips (grown by Judy Baker) to be photographed following the Annual Show. Clare Foster, Eric Hsu and Simon Wallis all read the manuscript and shared their feedback, for which I am very grateful. In addition, thanks to Matthew and Grete Smith who read and checked the Divisions section for me.

Anna Pavord has given encouragement and inspiration, and spent many tulip-filled days here at Blacklands. Thank you for gently pushing me out of the nest to fly on my own.

I owe a debt of gratitude to our former head gardener Hannah Gardner for indulging my tulip obsession, introducing me to the delights of species tulips and (still) helping me to construct the best combinations for container and perennial plantings. With Penny Philip, Judith Brotherton and Molly Noble, you formed a team to be reckoned with.

The baton has now been ably taken by our current head gardener, Andrew Wilson, assisted by Siwan Clarke and Andrew Kirby (who makes all our beautiful plant structures and supports). Watch out – now the book is finished there will be no stopping me in the garden!

Mick Sinnick and Russell Drake have watered, hoed, raked, strimmed and dug their way through the seasons whatever the weather, Steve Fenner has cut and coppiced, and Di Fenner has kept everything on track in the house while baking for Britain.

I would like to give thanks to my friend (and first-rate floral designer) Shane Connolly for championing British flowers and local, seasonal growers, and including me on the journey towards a more environmentally friendly floral world.

Holly Gavin, Sophie Eley, Fiona Haser Bizony, Chrissie Wiltshire and Lily Fitch have flowered with me over the years (there are traces of you in this book). You are all so talented and a joy to work with.

The Enthoven family lent me their cottage and their vases – thank you for your kindness.

I am hugely appreciative of the following individuals for accommodating my endless questions; your immense knowledge has been invaluable:

John Amand
Fran Baker at Chatsworth House
Saskia Bodegom at KAVB
Eric Breed of Wild Tulips
John Grimshaw
Matthé Spruit at Hortus Bulborum
Richard Wilford and Tom Freeth of Kew Gardens
Brett Wilson and Simon Wallis of Cambridge University
    Botanic Gardens
The Committee members of WNETS

Jane Maw of Graham Maw Christie Literary Agency provided expert advice to a first-time author, and Christin Geall generously helped me with the book proposal.

My parents Hylton and Charlotte Bayntun-Coward sadly died too young, but I hope my siblings Emma, Edward and Jo will enjoy this book on their behalf.

Finally, and most importantly, my love and appreciation go to my husband Ed and our four children, Evie, Hope, Artie and Iris, who keep me young(ish) and make me happy. I love you more than tulips. Or even Lettie (see p.212).

Phaidon Press Limited
2 Cooperage Yard
London E15 2QR

Phaidon Press Inc.
111 Broadway
New York, NY 10006

phaidon.com

First published 2024
All text © Polly Nicholson 2024
© 2024 Phaidon Press Limited

ISBN 978 1 83866 768 9

A CIP catalogue record for this book is available from
the British Library and the Library of Congress.

The publisher would like to thank Britt Willoughby Dyer for
the use of her photographs on the following pages: 46, 59t,
65b, 97, 109tr, 110tr, 110br, 113tl, 113bl, 113br, 114tr, 117bl, 117br, 123tr,
124tl, 127tl, 127bl, 132bl, 180–81, 242br. In addition, Clive Nichols
for his photograph on p.65 (top). All other photography by
Andrew Montgomery.

Commissioning Editor: Victoria Clarke
Project Editor: Victoria Clarke
Production Controller: Lily Rodgers

Designed by Lacasta Design

Printed on sustainable paper
from mixed sources

Printed in China

POLLY NICHOLSON is a tulip specialist, keen environmentalist
and the founder of Bayntun Flowers, a small organic flower
farm in Wiltshire, southwest England. Passionate about tulips,
she has been growing species, historic and annual garden
varieties for over fifteen years and holds the National Collection
of *Tulipa* (historic) with Plant Heritage. Nicholson grew up in the
countryside near Bath and read English literature with medieval
studies at the University of Exeter before obtaining a diploma
in horticulture from the English Gardening School at Chelsea
Physic Garden in 2003. Prior to establishing Bayntun Flowers,
she was an antiquarian book specialist at Sotheby's in London.
Nicholson is an active member of Flowers from the Farm, a
trustee of Benton End House & Garden in Suffolk and has acted
as horticultural adviser for several Phaidon publications.

Editorial Note:

The growing guides and gardening advice in this book are
based on the author's experience and the climate at Blacklands
in Wiltshire, UK, which is temperate (USDA hardiness zone 8).
Key dates are included as a guide. You may need to adapt these
and flowering times may also vary depending on where you live.

Tulip heights have been measured by the author at Blacklands.
The Tulip names have been checked against the KAVB database
and the RHS *Plant Finder*, and AGM details are correct according
to the RHS AGM lists 2023. *Flames and Feathers* has been used as
the primary reference for the chapter on English Florists' tulips.